eat

CHELSEA WINTER

Photography by Tam West

RANDOM HOUSE
NEW ZEALAND

RANDOM HOUSE

UK | USA | Canada | Ireland | Australia
India | New Zealand | South Africa | China

Random House is an imprint of the Penguin Random House group of companies,
whose addresses can be found at global.penguinrandomhouse.com.

First published by Penguin Random House New Zealand, 2017

1 3 5 7 9 10 8 6 4 2

Text © Chelsea Winter, 2017
Photography © Tam West, 2017

The moral right of the author has been asserted.

Photography by Tam West
Design by Helen Gilligan-Reid. Typesetting by Kate Barraclough © Penguin Random House New Zealand
Styling by Victoria Bell. Special thanks to: Rachel Carter for ceramics,
and Flotsam and Jetsam for the vintage ceramics.
Prepress by Image Centre Group
Printed and bound in China by RR Donnelley Asia Printing Solutions Ltd

A catalogue record for this book is available from the National Library of New Zealand.

ISBN 978-0-14-377126-5

penguin.co.nz

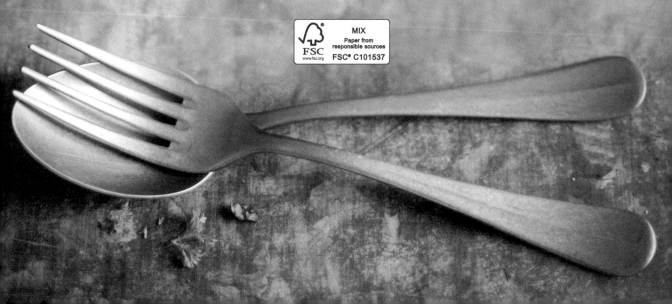

This book is dedicated to you,
the reader, with love.

welcome

Kia ora and welcome to *Eat*! It's taken me the best part of a year to write, test and photograph these recipes — all done rocking out in my kitchen at home. She's a pretty big job but I love every second of it — and when I'm in the zone, I'm not really just 'cooking'. I'm laughing, tasting, dancing, singing, flinging good energy around — and delicious food just sort of happens!

I'm often lost for words at the response I get from people using my cookbooks. The biggest thing for me is hearing people no longer need to rely on readymade stuff out of jars, pouches, packets and sachets — this is a big deal and it makes me so happy, because you honestly don't need that stuff! I'm here to help you cook real, tasty, exciting food that nourishes body and soul. Recipes made from scratch, using normal ingredients, that everyone can master at home.

I'm not too hung up on food trends, or the latest miracle diet they're telling us to try. I have a no-fuss, everyday approach to my food (I'm a low-fuss, everyday kind of person). What I am interested in is cooking for happiness — and making you look good in the kitchen!

You guys rock. Thank you for coming to say hi when you see me out and about, and for your emails, messages and posts to my Facebook page. I'm stoked that you take the time to connect with me — it always puts a smile on my dial. It's awesome to have you along with me on this delicious journey.

I hope you and your loved ones enjoy *Eat*. After all, I created it just for you.

Aroha nui,
Chelsea xx

PS — remember to eats loads of veges every day. Veges are your friend.

www.facebook.com/chelseawinterdelicious
@chelseawinter

contents

nourish

This section is the biggest, juiciest one in the book — and so it should be. Dinnertime is no small matter, and Nourish is dedicated to helping make the evening meal at your place delicious, stress-free and full of homemade goodness. Go ahead and take your pick from a huge variety of family-friendly recipes using chicken, beef, lamb, pork, seafood or sausages — as well as a few vegetarian dishes thrown in there for healthy balance. I've designed all the recipes so that anyone can make them, and with those feeding fussy eaters in mind (I'm sure that applies to more than a few of you). Yep, you'll be grilling, frying, steaming, roasting, baking and BBQing your way to utter scrumptiousness! You'll notice that the servings are generous, because whatever doesn't get eaten is meant to be kept for later. That's how it's always gone in my household — leftovers for lunch! Beats a crusty old sandwich any day.

Chicken Tikka Masala

Spice mix

2 tbsp ground paprika

1 tbsp ground turmeric

2 tsp ground cumin

2 tsp curry powder

2 tsp garam masala

½ tsp chilli powder

½ tsp finely ground black pepper

½ tsp finely ground white pepper

¼ tsp ground cloves

Curry

700g–1kg boneless chicken
thighs, chopped into 5cm
pieces

¾ cup unsweetened yoghurt

1 tbsp fresh lemon juice

50g butter (or 3 tbsp coconut or
grapeseed oil)

2 onions, finely chopped

6 cloves garlic, crushed

2 tbsp fresh ginger, finely
chopped

2 cups chicken stock

1 x 400g can chopped tomatoes
in purée

1 x 400ml can coconut milk

1 tbsp brown sugar

1 cinnamon stick, whole (optional)

1 bay leaf (optional)

fresh parsley or coriander, to
serve

shredded coconut, to serve

Chelsea's tips

♥ A BBQ is a nice way to grill
the chicken, as it imparts a
smoky flavour to the dish.
Start on an oiled hotplate and
finish on the grill.

PREP 10 MINUTES PLUS 1 HOUR MARINATING TIME
COOK 35 MINUTES   **SERVES** 6

This is a nice little twist on a chicken curry — the chicken is marinated
in spices and yoghurt for ultimate flavour and tenderness, then grilled
before it's added to the simmer sauce, so you get a nice subtle smokiness.
The marinating chicken can be left in the fridge for up to two days in
an airtight container — and the sauce can also be made ahead and
refrigerated, so it's just a matter of cooking the chicken and simmering it
in the sauce before serving.

Combine all the spices in a small bowl.

Place the chicken pieces in a mixing bowl with the yoghurt, lemon juice
and half of the spice mix. Cover and leave to marinate for an hour or
overnight — or for two nights!

Preheat the oven grill to high. Line a roasting or oven tray with foil.

Heat the butter or oil in a frying pan over a medium heat. Add the onion
and cook, stirring, for 15 minutes until soft and turning golden. Add the
garlic and ginger and cook for another couple of minutes. Sprinkle in the
remaining spice mix and stir for a minute — you may need a bit more
butter or oil if it's looking a bit dry.

Add the stock, tomatoes, coconut milk, brown sugar, cinnamon stick and
bay leaf (if using), and stir to combine. Simmer over a medium heat until
reduced by about half and thickened to a curry sauce consistency, 20–30
minutes. Turn off the heat.

Arrange the chicken pieces (not touching) on the lined tray. Grill near the
top of the oven for about 10–15 minutes, or until starting to blacken and
sizzle on top. Don't worry about turning the chicken over — just transfer it
to the sauce, and simmer for a few minutes until heated and the chicken is
cooked through.

If you think the sauce is too thick, you can thin it down with more stock or
water. Taste the sauce and season with salt and pepper if you need to.

Serve the chicken and sauce over cooked basmati rice. Sprinkle with fresh
herbs and coconut toasted lightly in a pan, and dot with a little yoghurt if
you like. Accompany with naan or fried wraps.

Keeps covered in the fridge for a few days or in the freezer for up to
6 months.

Chicken, Thyme & Mushroom Risotto

PREP 15 MINUTES **COOK** 45 MINUTES **SERVES** 6

4 cups salt-reduced chicken stock

500g boneless and skinless chicken thighs

neutral oil, e.g. avocado or grapeseed, for frying

¼ cup extra virgin olive oil

1 large onion, finely chopped

2 stalks celery, finely diced

1¾ cups Arborio or short-grain rice

⅔ cup white wine (sauvignon blanc, pinot gris or chardonnay)

350g Portobello or brown mushrooms, chopped

3 tbsp fresh thyme leaves, pulled off sprigs

¾ cup freshly grated Parmesan, plus extra to serve

75g butter, cubed

⅓ cup finely chopped fresh parsley

extra thyme or chopped parsley, to serve

squeeze of lemon juice (optional)

———

Chelsea's tips

♥ You can add a cup of thawed peas in the last few minutes of cooking if you like.

♥ Leave out the chicken for a meat-free meal.

This recipe is going to be popular — just a funny feeling I get. Fun fact: traditionally, Italians wouldn't put chicken in their risotto because they serve risotto as an entrée to be followed by the meaty main course (like the Golden Tuscan Chicken & Potatoes on page 38). However, here in NZ we eat it as a main and this is a one-pan dish, so it makes sense to have it all in there. It's a beautiful meal with subtle flavours and equally suitable for entertaining or just a weeknight treat.

Pour the stock into a medium-sized saucepan, cover and bring to a simmer (you'll add this to the risotto later). Turn the heat off and keep covered so it stays hot.

Arrange the chicken on a board and pat dry on both sides with paper towels. Cut into bite-sized pieces and season all over with salt and pepper.

Place 1 tablespoon of the frying oil in your largest frying pan over a high heat. When very hot, add the chicken and let it sizzle, without stirring, until browned on one side. Turn to brown the other side. Transfer to a bowl and set aside.

Pour the olive oil into the same pan and reduce the heat to medium-low. Add the onion and celery and cook for 10 minutes, stirring often, until softened and translucent.

Add the rice, increase the heat and cook for a couple of minutes, stirring with a wooden spoon to make sure the rice is evenly coated in oil. When the rice is very hot (but not browned), it should start to hiss and sizzle.

Pour in the wine, stir and let it bubble for another minute or so until the liquid has evaporated. Place the chicken back in the pan with the mushrooms and thyme. Reduce the heat to medium-low again.

Add a bit less than ½ cup (almost a ladleful) of the hot stock to the pan and let it simmer gently while you keep stirring with the wooden spoon/ shimmying the pan until the liquid is absorbed into the rice. Repeat this process until you've used all the stock — it should take 20–30 minutes. When the rice is cooked, it should be tender but still with a bit of an *al dente* bite in the centre. You want the risotto to be slightly wet and soupy rather than dry.

Add the Parmesan, butter and parsley and stir. Taste, and season with salt and pepper as desired. You probably need more than you think — there is a lot of rice there.

To serve, spoon into bowls and sprinkle with extra herbs and Parmesan. Add a squeeze of lemon if you like. Great served on its own or with a fresh salad and crusty bread.

Chicken Saltimbocca

4 skinless chicken breasts
cracked black pepper
16–24 sage leaves
8–10 slices prosciutto
½ cup plain flour
50g butter
2 tbsp olive oil
½ cup chicken stock
½ cup water
⅔ cup cream
1 tbsp lemon juice

___

PREP 10 MINUTES   **COOK** 15 MINUTES   **SERVES** 6–8

This is my version of an Italian dish that traditionally uses veal, but chicken is a nice substitute. Translated, *saltimbocca* means 'jumps in the mouth'. I like this, because if you're propelling food into your mouth so fast it seems like it's jumping in there itself, then it must be good. And, really, when have the Italians let us down in the food stakes? Never, that's when.

Preheat the oven to 60°C regular bake (to keep the chicken warm later). Have a medium-sized roasting tray ready.

Slice the chicken breasts in half lengthways through the thin side, so the two halves are as equal in thickness as possible. They should be 1.5cm thick or less. If not, place between two pieces of baking paper and bash them out with a rolling pin so they are a bit thinner. Season both sides with pepper.

Place a couple of sage leaves on one side of each piece of chicken. Wrap a piece of prosciutto around each piece of chicken — it's okay if the ends aren't covered. Stick any spare sage leaves onto the exposed chicken; they should stay on there.

Place the flour in a small bowl. Carefully dredge each piece of chicken to coat with flour, then clap the chicken between your hands a couple of times to dust off the excess flour — you only want a very thin dusting.

Heat the butter and oil in a large frying pan over a medium heat until the butter is melted and foaming, then add as many pieces of chicken as will comfortably fit. Cook for a few minutes until one side is golden brown, then turn to cook the other side. Set aside in the roasting tray, cover with foil and place in the preheated oven. Repeat with the remaining chicken.

Carefully pour the stock and water into the same frying pan, turn the heat up and simmer, stirring to dislodge all the yummy crusty brown bits from the bottom. Simmer rapidly until reduced by about half.

Add the cream and simmer rapidly for another few minutes until thickened into a nice pouring sauce. Stir in the lemon juice and season with pepper. Add any resting juices from the chicken back into the sauce, too.

Serve the chicken with the sauce (I have mine sitting in the sauce here but you can pour it on top), pasta, rice or potatoes and salad or veges.

Creamy Chicken & Mushroom Pasta

PREP 20 MINUTES   **COOK** 30 MINUTES   **SERVES** 4–6

4 cups dry penne (or similar pasta)

500g boneless and skinless chicken thighs

neutral oil, e.g. grapeseed, for frying

100g butter or ¼ cup olive oil

4 cloves garlic, crushed

1 tbsp fresh thyme leaves, pulled off sprigs

¼ cup dry white wine (optional)

300–400g button mushrooms, sliced

1½ cups cream

½ cup milk

2 tbsp Dijon mustard

1 tsp finely ground white or black pepper

1 cup frozen peas

1 cup ripe cherry tomatoes

¼ cup chopped fresh parsley

¾ cup freshly grated Parmesan or cheddar cheese

lemon wedges, to serve

Chelsea's tips

♥ If you don't like peas, stir in some chopped spinach towards the end of cooking — or serve steamed greens on the side.

It's undeniable that we Kiwis love a good creamy pasta. What's not to love? The creamy Chicken Fettucine in *Homemade Happiness* is one of my all-time most popular recipes — this is like its sister dish, quicker to make but still delicious. It's nice and easy to prepare, tasty and very filling. The cherry tomatoes you could leave out if you like, but they add a nice fresh pop in the mouth to thwart the creamy sauce. Be generous with herbs and lemon juice — fresh is best!

Just over half-fill your largest saucepan with water and add 1 teaspoon salt. Cover, bring to the boil, add the pasta, stir and boil, uncovered, for about 7 minutes, or until *al dente* (still firm to the bite). Drain, reserving ¼ cup of the cooking liquid, then add the pasta back to the saucepan and set aside.

Pat the chicken dry with paper towels, cut into bite-sized pieces and season all over with salt and pepper.

Heat a large frying pan over a high heat. When hot, add 1 tablespoon of the frying oil and the chicken. Leave to sizzle until golden and crispy on one side, then stir and brown the other side. Set aside in a bowl (it doesn't have to be cooked through yet).

Turn the heat down to medium under the same pan (don't rinse it). Add the butter or olive oil and, when it's foaming, add the garlic and thyme. Cook, stirring, for a couple of minutes until fragrant. If you like, you can add the wine now to deglaze the pan a bit.

Add the mushrooms and cook for another 5 minutes until softened.

Add the cooked chicken, cream, milk, mustard and pepper to the pan, stirring to combine evenly. Simmer for 5–10 minutes until the sauce has thickened to a pasta sauce consistency.

Add the peas, tomatoes, parsley and the reserved pasta water, and simmer for another minute or two.

Pour or spoon the chicken sauce into the saucepan with the pasta and stir to combine. Taste, and season with salt until you're happy with it (don't forget this step — it will need seasoning!).

Serve the pasta in bowls with a sprinkle of cheese, a squeeze of lemon juice and a crack of pepper.

Buffalo Chicken Burgers with Blue Cheese Sauce

1kg boneless chicken thighs
(skin-on or skinless)

¼ cup chipotle sauce (optional)

2 tbsp Tabasco sauce

1 tbsp paprika

1 tbsp ground coriander

¼ tsp chilli powder

2 tsp lemon juice

1 cup plain flour

1 tbsp finely ground white
pepper

1 tbsp finely ground black pepper

1 tbsp ground ginger

3 tsp salt

neutral oil, e.g. grapeseed, for
frying

6–8 burger buns or ciabatta rolls,
halved, toasted and buttered

salad fillers, e.g. grated carrot,
lettuce, sliced cucumber

Blue cheese sauce

1 cup mayonnaise

1 clove garlic, crushed

100g blue cheese, finely chopped

½ cup finely chopped parsley

1 tsp finely ground black pepper

2 stalks celery, finely chopped

Chelsea's tips

♥ The leftover blue cheese
sauce will last for a week in the
fridge — it's great for sandwiches
and goes well with BBQ'd
chicken and steak. Or even
tossed through cooked potatoes.
You may need to drain off any
watery liquid first.

♥ Try making the blue cheese
sauce with half sour cream and
half mayonnaise for a creamier
option.

PREP 20 MINUTES PLUS 30 MINUTES MARINATING TIME
COOK 10–15 MINUTES **SERVES** 5–6

Buffalo chicken nibbles with blue cheese sauce is one of my favourite foods of all time — there's a great recipe in *At My Table* for the traditional version. Now, four books later, I've taken it to burger form, and it really is exceptionally delicious. Even people who normally snub their nose at blue cheese will enjoy this sauce, I'd wager.

Place the chicken in a non-metallic mixing bowl with the chipotle sauce (if using), Tabasco sauce, paprika, coriander, chilli powder and lemon juice. Toss to combine evenly. Cover and leave for 30 minutes (or refrigerate overnight).

To make the blue cheese sauce, combine all the ingredients except the celery in a bowl. Cover and refrigerate until needed. When ready to use, stir through the celery (if you leave it in the sauce for too long, it leaches water and makes the sauce runny).

Remove the chicken from the fridge 30 minutes before cooking.

Add the flour, peppers, ginger and salt to a bowl and stir (you will probably sneeze here).

Grab a piece of chicken that's got a good coating of the marinade and scrunch it around in the flour mix until it has a craggy coating.

Pour 2cm oil into the bottom of a frying pan over a medium-high heat. When it's hot (it might need a few minutes), add the chicken and cook for 4–5 minutes each side until golden brown all over. Set aside to rest for 5 minutes before serving.

To serve, spread the blue cheese sauce on the bottom half of the toasted, buttered buns. Place the chicken and salad on top and finish with the top half of each bun.

Lemongrass & Ginger Chicken

800g–1kg boneless chicken thighs

⅓ cup lemongrass paste (or 4 stalks lemongrass)

¼ cup peanut oil or neutral oil, e.g. grapeseed

¼ cup roughly chopped fresh ginger

1 clove garlic

1 tbsp fish sauce

1 tsp ground cumin

1 tsp ground turmeric

1 cup chopped fresh coriander (leaves and stalks) and mint (or just coriander), plus extra for serving

zest and juice of 1 lime (or lemon)

1 kaffir lime leaf, very finely chopped (optional)

½ tsp finely ground white or black pepper

pinch chilli flakes (optional)

chopped fresh chilli, deseeded

sweet chilli sauce (optional)

extra lime or lemon juice (optional)

———

Chelsea's tips

♥ Kaffir lime leaves add a beautiful flavour to the marinade — you can find them at the supermarket or your local greengrocer.

PREP 10 MINUTES PLUS 3+ HOURS MARINATING TIME
COOK 15 MINUTES   **SERVES** 4

This is a gorgeous marinade that's bursting with fresh, tangy Vietnamese flavours. The chicken is lovely cooked on the BBQ as below, or you can cook it in a frying pan if the weather isn't playing nice. A drizzle of sweet chilli sauce and you're taking it down to taste-town.

Place the chicken in a non-metallic bowl for marinating.

If you're using lemongrass stalks, peel off the tough bright green outer leaves. Cut off the very hard base. Bash each stalk with the base of your knife to tenderise it and chop finely before it goes in the processor.

Put the lemongrass in a food processor along with the oil, ginger, garlic, fish sauce, cumin, turmeric, herbs, lime zest and juice, kaffir lime leaf (if using), pepper and chilli (if using). Process until you have a smooth paste — you'll probably need to scrape down the sides a few times. If you don't have a food processor, just mince everything as finely as you can.

Add the paste to the chicken and toss to coat. Cover and refrigerate for at least 3 hours or overnight — up to 2 days.

Remove the chicken from the fridge 30–60 minutes before cooking. Arrange on a plate and season both sides with salt.

Preheat a clean BBQ hotplate (or frying pan) to medium, and oil it. When hot, add the chicken pieces and leave to cook for about 5 minutes before turning to cook the other side for another 5 minutes. If you like, give it 30 seconds on each side on the preheated grill plate to get the char lines at the very end. Let the chicken rest, covered with foil, for 10 minutes before serving.

To serve, scatter with extra coriander and chopped fresh chilli, and a drizzle of sweet chilli sauce and lime juice if you like. Great served with the Asian Slaw on page 150.

Owen's Chicken & Kumara Pot Pie

700g orange kumara (or pumpkin)

2 onions, quartered

3 whole bulbs garlic, unseparated and unpeeled

2 stalks rosemary, leaves pulled off and chopped

¼ cup extra virgin olive oil

1kg boneless chicken thighs (or 1.5kg bone-in)

neutral oil, e.g. grapeseed, avocado or coconut, for frying

4 cups roughly chopped spinach (or silver beet with the white stalks removed)

25g butter

200g crème fraîche

1–2 sheets flaky puff pastry

1 free-range egg, lightly beaten with 1 tbsp milk (egg wash)

sesame or poppy seeds (optional)

___

Chelsea's tips

♥ This pie works beautifully with chicken drumsticks — but don't sear them, just roast for the whole time with the kumara. And leave the skins on!

PREP 1 HOUR **COOK** 40 MINUTES **SERVES** 6–8

This recipe is for a beloved friend of mine, who funnily enough isn't called Owen but Jean (a story I will tell you another day — it has to do with autocorrect, and a certain level of immaturity). I made a version of this pie for her at Great Barrier and at the same time promised I'd name a recipe after her. And so — ta-da! This pie is pretty awesomely tasty, and you can make the filling in advance and just assemble the pie when you're ready.

Preheat the oven to 180°C fan-bake. Have one large (or two medium) roasting trays ready.

Peel the kumara and cut into 4cm chunks. Place on one of the roasting trays with the broken-up onion, garlic bulbs and rosemary. Drizzle the veges with the olive oil. Toss to combine and season with salt and pepper.

Bake in the preheated oven for 25 minutes.

While the kumara is cooking, pat the chicken thighs dry with paper towels and season all over with salt and pepper. Place 1 tablespoon neutral oil in a frying pan over a high heat. When hot, add the chicken in two batches and sear for 1–2 minutes each side until golden all over. Transfer to a plate (leave the pan unwashed for later).

After the first 25 minutes is up for the veges, add the chicken and its juices to the same tray (just on top of the veg is fine) and roast everything for another 20 minutes. Remove from the oven and set aside to cool slightly.

Put the spinach or silver beet in the chicken frying pan with the butter and ¼ cup water. Place over a medium-high heat. Simmer until the spinach or silver beet is wilted and the liquid has mostly evaporated. Remove from the heat.

Chop or shred the chicken into bite-sized chunks. Reserve any pan juices.

Squeeze the garlic flesh out of the skins and add along with the chicken and veges to the frying pan (make sure you scrape up any brown crusty bits from the bottom of the roasting tray and add them, too — they are taste sensations!).

Stir through the crème fraîche to combine, and season to taste with salt and pepper. I like to mush the kumara up a bit so it's part of the sauce rather than just chunks.

Spoon the mixture either into one big pie dish or individual ramekins. Cut the pastry so it's just a little bit larger than your dish/es, and press it onto the rim of the dish to seal. Brush with the egg wash (sprinkle with sesame or poppy seeds if you like) and cut a couple of steam holes in the top.

Bake in the preheated oven for 30–40 minutes, or until dark golden brown on top. Serve with steamed greens or a salad.

Lightning Chicken
with Thyme Cream

PREP 5 MINUTES **COOK** 20 MINUTES **SERVES** 4–6

1kg chicken thighs (bone-in or boneless, skin-on or skinless)

neutral oil, e.g. grapeseed, for frying

25g butter

2 cloves garlic, crushed

⅓ cup white wine

1½ cups cream

1 tbsp chopped fresh thyme leaves

———

Why 'lightning' chicken? Because it's as quick as lightning to prepare! The trick is to make sure you get a good golden colour on the thighs when you sear them, because it's that colour that creates the flavour of the sauce.

Remove the chicken from the fridge 30–60 minutes before cooking. Pat the chicken dry with paper towels. Season on both sides with salt and pepper, being quite generous.

Heat 1–2 tablespoons of the oil in a large frying pan over a fairly high heat. When very hot, add the chicken (skin-side down if it has skin). You may need to do this in two batches — don't crowd the pan or the chicken might start stewing.

Leave the chicken to fry without turning until it has turned a deep golden brown colour on one side. Turn over and brown the other side. You can turn the chicken back over a couple of times to get it looking browner and crispier. Also, the more crusty brown stuff that builds up in the bottom of the pan, the better.

When both sides of the chicken are lovely and brown, set aside on a plate or roasting tray.

Tip any excess oil from the pan and replace over a medium heat. Add the butter and garlic and swish it around for 30 seconds. Add the wine, increase the heat to high, and let it bubble rapidly for about 30–60 seconds to evaporate the alcohol — it should reduce by about half.

Stir in the cream and thyme, then add the chicken and any resting juices. Reduce the heat to medium-high and let everything simmer until the chicken is cooked through and the sauce has reduced down to a nice consistency — not too thick; it's quite a rich sauce. If it becomes too thick, simply add more cream and simmer again until you're happy with it. Season to taste with salt and pepper.

Serve with steamed greens and mash, new potatoes, pasta, bulghur wheat or rice.

BBQ Peri-Peri Chicken

1 size 14–16 chicken (free-range is preferable)

neutral oil, e.g. grapeseed, for grilling

fresh lime or lemon wedges, to serve

Chilli oil

½ cup neutral oil, e.g. grapeseed

1 tbsp chilli flakes

Marinade

6 cloves garlic, crushed

1 tbsp paprika

2 tsp lemon juice

2 tsp chilli powder

1 tsp ground turmeric

1 tsp ground ginger

1 tsp finely ground black pepper

1 tsp finely ground white pepper

——

Chelsea's tips

♥ If you're serving a crowd, use two smaller chickens rather than one big one — and double the marinade.

PREP 20 MINUTES PLUS 6+ HOURS MARINATING TIME
COOK 1 HOUR 15 MINUTES **SERVES** 4–5

Barbecued chicken is so delicious, but it can be awkward — too dry in some spots and raw in others. My trick is to first cook the chicken very gently in the oven, then just finish it on the BBQ for the lovely smoky flavour and charred look. It's a no-fail system! If you're not a fan of chilli, you might want to leave out the chilli powder and oil. Me, I love chilli and this offers a good kick!

To make the chilli oil, combine the oil and chilli flakes in a small saucepan and cook gently over a medium-low heat for 20 minutes. Leave to cool and store in an airtight container.

To butterfly the chicken, pat dry all over with paper towels. Turn the chicken breast-side down on a board. Hold the tail firmly and use kitchen scissors (or a sharp knife) to snip down one side of the backbone all the way to the end, cutting right through the small rib bones. Do the same for the other side, then discard the backbone. Snip off any excess skin from the ends. Turn the chicken over and flatten by pressing down on the breast with your palm.

Slash a couple of deep cuts into the legs, thighs and breast, right down to the bone.

Mix the marinade ingredients together in a bowl (or use a small food processor). Rub all over the chicken, using it all up. Place in a resealable bag or covered dish and leave to marinate for at least 6 hours or overnight.

Remove the chicken from the fridge an hour before cooking.

Preheat the oven to 120°C regular bake. Line a roasting dish with baking paper and place the chicken in the dish.

Bake in the preheated oven for 1 hour. This will cook the chicken just about all the way through, as long as it's been out of the fridge for an hour first.

Preheat a clean BBQ grill to a medium-high heat. Brush with oil.

Brush the chicken on both sides with oil and season all over with salt. Carefully place over the preheated grill and leave to cook without disturbing it for 5–10 minutes.

Turn the chicken over and cook for another 5 minutes. Transfer to a board, cover loosely with foil and rest for 15 minutes before slicing.

To serve, I chop the chicken up into chunks to make it easier. Season all over again with salt and pepper. Let people drizzle their own chilli oil on top, and squeeze on some fresh lime or lemon. Serve with your choice of salad or vegetables, and rice or potatoes.

Crummy Chicken

1–1.5kg chicken drumsticks

2–3 cups breadcrumbs
(storebought or make your
own, see page 168)

½ tsp salt

¼ cup chopped fresh herbs
(thyme, sage, oregano,
rosemary)

¼ cup extra virgin olive oil, plus
extra for drizzling

3 free-range eggs

⅓ cup flour

½ tsp finely ground black pepper

½ tsp finely ground white pepper

1 tsp salt

Chelsea's tips

♥ These make delicious picnic or
lunchbox fodder when they are
cold.

PREP 10 MINUTES **COOK** 45 MINUTES **SERVES** 4–6

Sounds appetising, eh? Mike requested this one, as apparently crumbed
drumsticks were his favourite thing growing up. Not only are drumsticks
more affordable, they have loads of flavour and cooked like this, the meat
is juicy and tender. No need for a deep-fryer here — you get perfect,
crunchy, oven-baked chicken that'll have people coming back for seconds
(and thirds!).

Preheat the oven to 180°C fan-bake (200°C regular bake). Line a roasting
tray with baking paper.

Lay the drums on a clean board. Pat dry with paper towels. If the skins have
sagged down, pull them back up to cover the meat.

Tip the crumbs into a large bowl (a roasting tray also works well) with ½ tsp
salt. Add the chopped herbs and oil and toss to combine.

Crack the eggs into a medium bowl and whisk until smooth.

Place the flour, peppers and 1 tsp salt in a plastic bag and shake to
combine. Add the chicken (in batches if you need to) and shake in the bag
to coat evenly.

Dip each floured drumstick in the egg wash, let the excess egg drip off for
a few seconds, then place in the bowl of crumbs and pack the crumb on as
well as you can.

Arrange the crumbed drums in the lined roasting tray (not touching).
Drizzle or brush them all with more olive oil.

Bake in the preheated oven for 35 minutes. Then turn the oven up 20°C
and bake drums for another 10–15 minutes to get them really brown and
crispy. If you like, you can drizzle or brush more olive oil over while cooking,
too. You can turn the drums over while cooking, but it's not essential.

These go with pretty much anything you feel like — in summer with
a nice salad and Crunchy Potato Wedges (see page 138), or in winter
with steamed greens and the Kumara & Caramelised Onion Mash from
page 136.

Sticky Honey-Soy Nibbles

1kg chicken nibbles
½ cup soy sauce
⅓ cup honey
2 tbsp peanut oil
2 tbsp sweet chilli sauce
2 tsp malt or white vinegar
½ tsp sesame oil
pinch chilli flakes
⅓ cup water
1 tbsp cornflour mixed with
    2 tbsp water
2 tbsp sesame seeds
2–3 spring onions, chopped (or
    ¼ cup chopped fresh chives)

___

Chelsea's tips

♥ If you don't have time to
   marinate the nibbles, it's not
   the end of the world. They'll
   still be super tasty!

PREP 10 MINUTES PLUS 2+ HOURS MARINATING TIME
COOK 40 MINUTES **SERVES** 4 AS A SNACK

The benchmark of a good chicken nibble marinade is that when it gets all over your face and fingers, a wet cloth or running water is required — dry napkins just won't cut it. This is a quick, tasty little dish — and you can forget about jars of pre-made marinades, homemade is best! As a meal, serve with rice and a salad (the Asian Slaw on page 150 would be perfect) or steamed greens.

Pat the chicken nibbles dry with paper towels.

Place the soy sauce, honey (you need to warm it for 20 seconds in the microwave if it's firm), peanut oil, sweet chilli sauce, vinegar, sesame oil and chilli flakes in a large non-metallic bowl or plastic container. Whisk to combine, add the chicken, toss, cover and refrigerate for at least 2 hours or overnight.

Preheat the oven to 180°C fan-bake and set a rack in the centre of the oven. Line a large roasting tray with baking paper.

Drain and reserve the marinade, and transfer the nibbles to the lined roasting tray, not touching if possible.

Pour the leftover marinade into a small saucepan and add the water, and the cornflour/water mixture. Simmer over a medium heat for a few minutes until thickened. Remove from the heat and brush a layer onto the nibbles.

Bake the nibbles in the centre of the oven for about 40 minutes, brushing them with the thickened marinade 4–5 times during cooking. Watch they don't burn — turn the oven down if you think it's too hot. Sprinkle with sesame seeds halfway through cooking.

Serve with a few chopped spring onions or chives.

Chicken Cramembert Melts

PREP 20 MINUTES   **COOK** 20 MINUTES PLUS RESTING TIME
SERVES 6

1kg chicken breasts

¼ cup extra virgin olive oil

1 onion, finely chopped

6 cloves garlic, finely chopped or
  crushed

½ cup chopped fresh herbs
  (thyme, rosemary, oregano,
  sage)

1 x 375ml jar cranberry sauce

1 cup chicken stock

¼ cup tomato paste

1 tbsp Dijon mustard

1 tbsp red or white wine vinegar

½ tsp finely ground white or black
  pepper

pinch chilli flakes (optional)

½ cup cream cheese

125g Camembert or Brie, sliced

½ cup dried cranberries

zest of 1 lemon

———

Chelsea's tips

♥ Skin-on chicken is nice if you
  can find it.

In case you're wondering, 'cramembert' is not a typo, it's another Chelsea-ism — a hybrid of Camembert and cranberries and quite a horrible-sounding word, really. But you know me and my cringey puns! Anyway, this meal is anything but horrible — in fact, I wouldn't be surprised if it was one of the book favourites. Creamy Camembert, tangy cranberry and a lovely savoury sauce make for a juicy, chin-dribbling dinner that'll have them clambering across the table for more.

Preheat the oven to 220°C regular bake and have a baking tray or dish ready. Remove the chicken from the fridge 20–30 minutes before cooking.

Pat the chicken skin dry with paper towels and season the breasts all over with salt and pepper. Set aside on a chopping board.

Add the olive oil and onion to a frying pan over a medium heat, and cook for about 5 minutes, stirring often, until golden (don't let the onion burn or crisp up). Stir in the garlic and most of the herbs (leave some for stuffing the chicken) and cook for another few minutes.

To the pan, add the cranberry sauce, chicken stock, tomato paste, mustard, vinegar, pepper and chilli (if using). Stir to dissolve the cranberry sauce and then simmer over a medium-high heat for 5–10 minutes, or until thickened.

While the sauce is simmering, cut each chicken breast through the middle of the long edge (not quite all the way through) so it can be opened up a bit like a hamburger bun, leaving one of the long edges as a sort of hinge. Spread the inside with some cream cheese, then layer with some Camembert or Brie, cranberries and remaining herbs. Sprinkle with lemon zest. Fold over and seal shut with toothpicks (you can also use snipped rosemary stalks).

Pour the sauce into the bottom of the baking dish, then nestle the chicken breasts in. Scatter any leftover dried cranberries in. Give everything a drizzle with olive oil and a crack of salt and pepper.

Bake in the preheated oven for 15–17 minutes, depending on how big the chicken breasts are. Remove from the oven and, if you can, allow to rest for 10 minutes before serving with pasta or potatoes and your favourite steamed vegetables.

King Creole Chicken & Grilled Pineapple Salsa

500g boneless chicken thighs

Marinade

¼ cup neutral oil, e.g. grapeseed

3 tbsp paprika

1½ tbsp dried oregano

1½ tbsp lemon juice

1 tbsp fresh chopped thyme
  leaves (or 2 tsp dried)

5 cloves garlic, crushed

2 tsp Worcestershire sauce

1 tsp finely ground white pepper

1 tsp finely ground black pepper

½ tsp chilli powder

1 tsp salt

Salsa

3 red capsicums

½ fresh pineapple

½ cup finely chopped red onion

1 large avocado, chopped

2 tbsp finely chopped mint,
  coriander, basil or parsley

1 tbsp brown sugar

1 tbsp lime or lemon juice

_____

Chelsea's tips

♥ You don't have to grill the
  pineapple or the capsicum if you
  don't want to — just cut up raw
  and add to the salsa.

PREP 15 MINUTES PLUS 6+ HOURS MARINATING TIME
COOK 20 MINUTES **SERVES** 4–5

Have you heard Elvis's song 'King Creole'? It's pretty cool, just like this dish. (Not really relevant, but I listened to Elvis a lot while I was writing and testing this book.) This is extremely tasty chicken that you can marinate in advance and have ready to go when you need it. The salsa is a party in the mouth — zingy, sweet, salty with fresh flavours and a nice texture going on. It's designed to be more like a salad to go with the chicken, rather than a sauce.

Place the marinade ingredients in a medium bowl and stir to combine.

Lay the chicken on a clean board and pat dry all over with paper towels. Slice into bite-sized chunks, add to the marinade and toss to combine. Cover and refrigerate for at least 6 hours or overnight.

Remove the chicken from the fridge about 30 minutes before cooking. Thread onto kebab skewers (soak them in water first if they are wooden).

Grill the capsicums whole on the BBQ over a high heat (or use the oven) until they are totally black and charred all over. Set aside in a plastic bag and twist shut.

Cut the pineapple into 1.5cm slices. Cut off the skin and discard. Season the pineapple all over with salt and pepper.

Preheat a clean BBQ grill to medium and brush with oil. Add the pineapple and cook for a few minutes each side until coloured all over and tender. Transfer to a chopping board and cut into dice. Place in a serving bowl with the onion.

Peel the skin off the capsicums, and discard along with the stalk and seeds. Cut the flesh into pieces and add to the pineapple. Just before serving, stir through the avocado, herbs, sugar and juice, and season to taste with salt and pepper.

To cook the chicken kebabs, brush a clean BBQ grill or hotplate with oil and turn on to a medium heat. Place the kebabs on the grill and cook until browned all over and cooked through — about 7–10 minutes. Remove from the heat and transfer to a roasting tray. Cover lightly with foil to rest for 10 minutes before serving.

Serve the chicken with the salsa on the side, with a squeeze of fresh lime juice if you like. Great with a salad or slaw, and fresh rolls or grilled wraps.

Golden Tuscan Chicken & Potatoes

PREP 15 MINUTES   **COOK** 45 MINUTES   **SERVES** 4–5

4–5 chicken Marylands (thigh with the leg attached) or bone-in thighs (skin must be on)

1kg Agria potatoes, scrubbed and chopped into 3cm chunks

½ cup extra virgin olive oil

4 stalks rosemary, leaves pulled off and chopped

5 cloves garlic, crushed

sea salt and pepper

Gravy

1½ cups chicken stock or water

3 tbsp plain flour mixed with ⅓ cup water

———

I had something similar to this when I was visiting Sorrento in Italy. The only problem was, it was the FOURTH course, so by the time it came out no one could eat it! I actually had to undo my jeans all the way to give it a proper go, as it was just too good not to eat. It's a very simple but extremely tasty dish — the chicken skin goes beautifully crispy and golden, and the fat renders out into the tray and helps to make the potatoes extra delicious. You get all the best things about roast chicken without the hassle of making roast chicken!

Preheat the oven to 200°C fan-bake and have two metal roasting trays ready.

Pat the chicken skin dry with paper towels. Place along with the potatoes on the trays.

Add the olive oil to a jug with the rosemary and garlic, and stir. Pour over the chicken and potatoes, then give it all a good toss and turn with your hands so everything is well and evenly coated in the oil — this is important. Leave the chicken skin-side up.

Season everything generously with sea salt and pepper — more salt than you would normally use, especially on the chicken skin, as it helps crisp it up.

Bake in the preheated oven for 45 minutes. Baste everything a few times during cooking (use a pastry brush or a spoon) with the oil from the base of the tray. You should also swap the trays around halfway through cooking so it cooks evenly. You can turn the potatoes once in the second half of cooking if you like.

It's ready when the skin of the chicken is a deep golden brown, and very crispy. The potatoes should be golden, too, and the bases will be crispy. You can grill it at the end of cooking to get it really nice and browned.

Transfer the chicken and potatoes to a warmed platter or tray (you can drizzle the cooking oil over top) while you make the gravy.

Place the roasting tray over a medium heat and add the chicken stock or water, and flour mixture, stirring all the time. Cook for 5 minutes until thickened — add more water if you need to. Make sure you scrape up all the caramelised chicken bits on the bottom with a wooden spoon or fish slice. Serve the chicken and potatoes with gravy and your choice of greens.

Incrediburgers

Patties

2 rashers streaky bacon

1kg beef mince (not lean or premium mince — just the standard stuff. Or make your own — see Chelsea's tips)

⅓ cup panko crumbs (or dried breadcrumbs)

2 tbsp tomato paste

1½ tsp Worcestershire sauce

1 tbsp Dijon mustard

1 clove garlic, crushed

1 tsp finely ground black pepper

Pickled red onion

2 red onions, sliced into rings

1 tsp salt

2 tsp lemon juice

Burgers

4–6 slices streaky bacon (optional)

4–6 burger buns, halved and buttered

To serve

sliced cheddar cheese

mayonnaise or aïoli

hot English mustard

ketchup (see page 164)

sliced gherkins or pickles

Chelsea's tips

♥ Mince for hamburger patties is easy to make at home if you have a meat grinder (some cake-mixer-type machines have an attachment you can buy). Chuck steak is your best bet as it has good fat content. Alternatively, you can finely chop the meat (and fat) and pulse to a coarse mince in a food processor in batches.

PREP 25 MINUTES **COOK** 15–20 MINUTES PLUS RESTING TIME **SERVES** 4–6

Burgers like you've never had before! The patties might seem a little different than the ones you're used to — there's no egg, onion or even herbs to pad them out. This is just a pure beef patty that delivers juiciness, flavour and meaty grunt (sorry). The burgers are best left simple with the added super-savoury flavours of red onion, condiments, cheese and gherkin — you could add lettuce if you like some crunch. You don't have to use the BBQ for this, but it does add a lovely smoky flavour.

In a frying pan, cook the first 2 rashers of bacon over a low heat for 5–10 minutes, until cooked but not coloured. Chop finely, allow to cool and place in a large mixing bowl.

Add the remaining patty ingredients to the bowl and gently combine with clean hands. Shape into 4–6 patties, arrange on a tray or plate, cover and refrigerate until you need them. Remove from the fridge 30–60 minutes before cooking.

Place the red onion, salt and lemon juice in a non-metallic bowl and toss to combine. Leave to sit for at least 15 minutes, or until needed. When ready to serve, squeeze the excess liquid out of the onion.

Preheat a clean BBQ grill or hotplate (or just use a frying pan) to a medium heat. Brush with oil and add the bacon (if using). Cook, turning, until crispy. Set aside and keep warm.

Just before you cook the patties, brush both sides with oil and season each side generously with salt, and extra cracked pepper if you like. Don't forget this step!

Preheat the BBQ hotplate and grill to a medium-high heat. Place the patties on the hotplate and cook for a few minutes. Turn over and cook for another few minutes, or until cooked to medium-well (keep the turning to a minimum if you can).

Brush the grill with oil and add the patties so they get a bit of a grilling and some flare-up as the juices hit the flames — just a minute or two should do it. If you like, you can place the cheese slices on top of the patties when they are almost done so they begin to melt.

Set the patties aside on a board or tray, loosely covered with foil, to rest for 5–10 minutes before serving.

Place the bun halves, butter-side down, on the grill and toast lightly before serving.

To serve, spread condiments of your choice on the bun bottoms, top with a patty, cheese and bacon, add gherkins and pickled onion, and finish with the top half of each bun.

Bali Beef Rendang

PREP 15 MINUTES **COOK** 1 HOUR **SERVES** 4–6

1kg rump steak

3 tbsp peanut oil

6 cloves garlic

3 shallots, peeled and chopped

4 large red chillies, deseeded and chopped

½ tsp chilli powder

3 tbsp roughly chopped fresh ginger

1½ tbsp ground turmeric

400ml coconut cream

400ml beef stock (reduced-salt is good)

1 tbsp ground cumin

2 tbsp soy sauce

2 tbsp brown sugar

2 kaffir lime leaves (or 2 bay leaves)

3 stalks lemongrass, white part only (or 3 tbsp lemongrass paste)

zest of 1 lime

½ tsp finely ground white or black pepper

1 tbsp fresh lime juice, plus extra if needed

———

THIS RECIPE IS EPIC! I went to Bali for the first time in 2016 and fell madly in love with everything about it (except the inebriated tourists) — but *especially* the food. I tasted this incredible beef rendang at the place I was staying, cooked by a local chef. They very kindly gave me the recipe — I had to amend it a bit to suit what's available here, but it's still bloody good! The interesting thing about rendang is that it's designed to keep without spoiling for a long time; the dry nature of the curry and the spices preserve the meat. I've kept leftovers in the fridge for 2 weeks and they tasted even better reheated.

Trim any excess fat and sinew from the beef and discard. Slice the beef into thin (5mm) strips.

Add the oil to a heavy-based frying pan over a medium heat. Add the garlic, shallots, chillies, chilli powder, ginger and turmeric. Cook, stirring, for 5 minutes until softened.

Transfer the mixture to a food processor with ¼ cup of the coconut cream. Let it cool for 5 minutes before processing to a paste.

Add the paste back to the pan along with the beef, stock, remaining coconut cream, cumin, soy sauce, sugar, kaffir lime leaves (or bay leaves), whole lemongrass stalks (or paste), lime zest and pepper. Stir to combine.

Leave it to simmer over a low heat — it should be bubbling, but not a frantic simmer; just a light simmer. Stir every now and then. The aim here is to let most of the liquid evaporate — it might take 30–60 minutes. You really do need to be paying attention when it starts to reduce right down, because if you forget about it, it will burn. Keep watch and keep stirring towards the end until you're happy with the consistency — a little bit of juiciness is okay but it's meant to be quite a dry curry, traditionally.

Remove the lemongrass stalks before serving. Add the lime juice, and taste it — you can add more salt, pepper, chilli or lime if you think it needs it. Serve with rice and steamed Asian greens, broccoli or beans.

Steak with Café de Paris Butter

5–6 steaks — scotch fillet, sirloin, eye fillet, rump

Café de Paris butter

200g butter, chopped

2 tbsp Dijon mustard

2 tbsp chopped shallot

1½ tbsp capers

1 tbsp chopped fresh dill (or 1 tsp dried)

2 tsp chopped fresh rosemary

1 tsp dried marjoram

1 tsp dried tarragon

1 tsp Worcestershire sauce

1 tsp salt

2 cloves garlic

1 anchovy, minced

½ tsp paprika

½ tsp curry powder

¼ cup chopped fresh parsley

——

Chelsea's tips

♥ If you don't have a food processor, you can finely mince everything by hand and either whip together with a wooden spoon or try to use an egg beater.

♥ The butter will keep in an airtight container in the fridge for a couple of weeks (make sure it's properly airtight) or in the freezer for a few months.

PREP 10 MINUTES   **COOK** 10 MINUTES PLUS RESTING TIME
SERVES 5–6

Classic Café de Paris butter is just so ingenious, and I seriously think it will change the way you eat steak forever! The best part about it is that it doesn't matter what cut you've got — rump, sirloin, scotch, eye fillet — just fry it until cooked to your liking and let this incredible buttery hero take it to new and amazing places. The recipe makes quite a bit, so you can always have some on hand when you want to jazz up your meat and three veg. Yep, it's terrific on chicken and pork, too.

You want the butter to be soft enough to process, but not melted. On a warm day just take it out of the fridge and chop 20 minutes before you begin. In winter, you could chop and microwave on the defrost setting in 20-second increments until it's softish, but not melty.

Add all the café de Paris butter ingredients to a food processor and process until well combined — you will need to run a spatula around the sides a few times and poke stubborn bits down to get it evenly mixed.

Scrape out of the processor onto a piece of wax paper, and form into a sausage shape — whatever thickness you like, really. Mine was about 5cm in diameter. Twist the ends up to seal as best you can, then wrap well again, or place in an airtight container and refrigerate. If air gets in when it's in the fridge, it will affect the taste of the butter.

Remove the steaks from the fridge 30 minutes before cooking. Pat dry with paper towels and rub generously with neutral oil on both sides. Season both sides with salt and pepper.

Heat a frying pan (or BBQ hotplate in summer) over a high heat. When hot, lightly oil the pan and add the steaks. Cook for a few minutes — how long really depends on the thickness of the steak. When one side is browned and crispy, turn over to cook the other side. The steak is medium-rare when it feels soft but with some springy, firm resistance. Really mushy is rare and getting firmer is heading towards well done!

Set aside to rest, loosely covered with foil, for 10 minutes. Slice butter about 5mm thick and place on top of the steaks so it melts into them.

Serve with your choice of sides — check out the Mix + Match chapter, starting on page 132.

Mamma Mia Meatball Bake

Meatballs

500g beef mince

500g pork mince (or make your own by mincing pork belly meat)

1 onion, minced

1 free-range egg

½ cup finely minced parsley

½ cup dried breadcrumbs (or use rolled oats or process crackers to a fine crumb)

3 tbsp tomato paste

3 cloves garlic, crushed

1 tsp salt

½ tsp finely ground white or black pepper

extra virgin olive oil, for frying

Sauce/topping

2 x 400g cans chopped tomatoes in purée

1 punnet ripe cherry tomatoes (optional)

⅓ cup tomato paste

1 tbsp chopped fresh rosemary leaves

6 cloves garlic, crushed

2 tsp balsamic vinegar

2 tsp dried oregano

3 tsp sugar

½ tsp fennel seeds (optional)

pinch chilli flakes

1 cup mozzarella chunks

1 cup freshly grated Parmesan

chopped parsley or fresh basil, to serve (optional)

———

PREP 20 MINUTES **COOK** 50 MINUTES **SERVES** 6–7

I have a bad habit of saying 'mamma mia!' incessantly after I've spent time in Italy (it sort of translates to 'oh my goodness'). It drives Mike bonkers. But it sums up how I feel about this dish, and this photo, too — it makes me want to dive into the saucy goodness! The good thing about baking meatballs like this is that you can have it all in the dish ready to go a few hours (or even a day) ahead of time, then just pop it in the oven when you're ready to serve with no frying or mess.

Place all the meatball ingredients except the oil in a large mixing bowl. Use clean hands to scrunch and mix until combined. Shape into quite large meatballs — about the size of a small apple. Set aside.

Combine the canned tomatoes, cherry tomatoes (if using), tomato paste, rosemary, garlic, vinegar, oregano, sugar, fennel seeds (if using) and chilli flakes in a very large baking dish. Season to taste with salt and pepper, and stir to combine.

Heat 2 tablespoons of the oil in a large frying pan over a medium-high heat. When hot, add half the meatballs and cook to brown all over. Transfer to the baking dish so they are sitting nestled in the sauce, and repeat with the remaining meatballs. At this point you can cover and refrigerate until needed.

Preheat the oven to 180°C regular bake (160°C fan-bake).

Bake in the preheated oven for 35 minutes, turning the meatballs once during cooking. Remove the dish, increase the oven temperature to 200°C, sprinkle the chunks of mozzarella and grated Parmesan on top, and return to the oven for 10 minutes to melt the cheese.

Serve with pasta, rice, potatoes, polenta or couscous, and steamed greens on the side. Sprinkle with chopped parsley or torn fresh basil leaves if you like.

Saucy Noodle Stir-fry

PREP 15 MINUTES **COOK** 10 MINUTES **SERVES** 5–6

700g rump or sirloin steak, cut
into strips

peanut, avocado or grapeseed
oil for frying

2 onions, roughly chopped

1 carrot, peeled and chopped

3 stalks celery, roughly chopped

5 cloves garlic, roughly chopped
or crushed

3 tsp finely grated or chopped
fresh ginger

1–2 large red chillies, chopped
(or a big pinch chilli flakes)

400g soft stir-fry noodles

1 head broccoli, chopped into
small florets

3 spring onions, chopped (or
1 bunch chives, chopped)

½ cup roasted peanuts or
cashews, to serve (optional)

Sauce

½ cup soy sauce

⅓ cup water or chicken stock

2 tbsp oyster sauce

1½ tbsp cornflour mixed with
2 tbsp water

1 tbsp brown sugar

2 tsp sesame oil

1 tsp white vinegar

¾ tsp finely ground white or black
pepper

―――

Chelsea's tips

♥ Use chicken or seafood in the
place of beef if you like.

I was home alone one night watching a movie when the actors began eating some sort of delicious-looking noodle thing out of those cardboard 'take-out' boxes. I suddenly had a hankering, so I immediately paused the movie, jumped up in my pyjamas and made this. Cripes, it was good! Everything you need is there in the one pan and it's as easy as anything to make.

If you have time, get the meat out of the fridge 30 minutes before you cook it.

Combine the sauce ingredients in a jug and have at the ready.

Heat a wok or your largest frying pan over a high heat. Season the meat all over with salt and pepper.

When the pan is searing hot, add 2 tablespoons of the frying oil and half the meat. Leave to sizzle until browned, then set aside. Repeat with the remaining meat.

Place the onion and carrot in the pan. Cook for a few minutes, then add the celery and cook for another couple of minutes. Toss in the garlic, ginger and chilli and stir-fry for another minute.

Add the noodles and broccoli and stir-fry for another minute.

Tip the meat and the resting juices back into the pan.

Stir the sauce ingredients, then pour into the pan. Cook for a few minutes, stirring occasionally, until the noodles are hot, the veges are tender and the sauce is thick and shiny.

Before serving, sprinkle with spring onions and the nuts (if using).

Rolls Royce of Roast Beef

1.25–2kg whole eye fillet

2 onions, chopped

olive oil

2 stalks fresh rosemary, leaves
    pulled off

1 bay leaf

Savoury coating

1½ tbsp olive oil

7 cloves garlic, crushed

2 tbsp Dijon mustard

4 anchovies, finely chopped
    (optional but you should use
    them)

2 tsp hot English mustard

2 tsp grated horseradish

2 tsp salt

1½ tsp finely ground black
    pepper

1 tsp brown sugar

1 tsp malt vinegar

Gravy

1 cup red wine (merlot or
    cabernet sauvignon)

1 cup beef stock

1 tbsp cornflour mixed with
    ¼ cup water

———

Chelsea's tips

♥ Any leftover meat can be sliced
and combined with the gravy,
then reheated together for
another meal the next night.

PREP 15 MINUTES **COOK** 40–55 MINUTES PLUS 20 MINUTES
RESTING TIME **SERVES** 5–10

As you know, I'm a fan of the cheaper, gruntier, more flavoursome cuts —
my books are full of them. But sometimes for a special occasion, a soft,
velvety piece of perfectly cooked eye fillet is just what you feel like. Ask
your butcher to cut you a reasonably even-sized piece so you don't have
to contend with a whole eye fillet which is huge at one end and thin at the
other. The peppery, mustardy coating adds something a little bit special.

Remove the meat from the fridge an hour or two before cooking. Remove
it from the packaging and pat dry with paper towels.

Preheat the oven to 220°C fan-bake.

Place the chopped onions in a roasting dish (ideally one that's just a little
bigger than the size of your meat) with a splash of olive oil, and toss to
coat. Add the rosemary leaves and bay leaf. Sit the beef on top.

Combine the coating ingredients together in a bowl (or use a processor),
then spread all over the beef in a good thick layer. Season all over with salt.

Transfer the beef to the oven, and turn the oven down immediately to
200°C regular bake.

Bake for about 11 minutes per 500g for medium-rare.

Remove from the oven, transfer the beef to a board or tray and cover
loosely (not tightly) with foil. Leave to rest for 20 minutes (don't skip this
step, or you'll compromise the quality of the whole roast — all the juice will
run everywhere when sliced).

Place the roasting dish (provided it's metal) on the stovetop over a
medium-high heat. Alternatively, pour the juices, onion and any crusty bits
into a saucepan. Add the wine and boil for 30 seconds to evaporate the
alcohol. Scrape up all the crusty bits from the bottom.

Pour the stock and the cornflour mixture into the gravy pan and simmer
for about 5 minutes. You don't want it to be thick and gluggy, so don't be
scared to thin it down with more wine, stock or water if needed. If it's too
thin, keep simmering to reduce it.

Add any resting juices from the meat to the gravy. Strain through a sieve
(discard the onions and herbs) and transfer to a serving jug.

Slice the beef and serve with the gravy. This goes beautifully with My
Famous Crunchy Roast Potatoes or my Cheesy Potato & Herb Bake, both
from *Homemade Happiness*. It's also great with the Kumara & Caramelised
Onion Mash on page 136, and the Big Roasted Veges on page 140.

Pork, Sage & Apple Pie with Kumara Topping

PREP 20 MINUTES **COOK** 3 HOURS **SERVES** 6–8

This recipe will have them coming back for seconds and thirds! Not at all difficult to make and combines beautiful flavours that work in perfect harmony. The dish has a warming, autumnal French-style vibe — herbs, apple, leek, garlic, butter, bacon and tender pork — you can't lose, I'm telling you! If you like, you can make this as a traditional pie with a puff pastry top and/or bottom.

Preheat the oven to 140°C regular bake.

Trim the excess fat from the pork shoulder (a little bit for flavour is okay), then cut the meat into 5cm chunks. Pat dry with paper towels and season well all over with salt and pepper.

Heat some oil in a frying pan over a high heat (or use a stovetop-safe casserole dish for this whole process if you have one). When it's very hot, add the pork. Fry without turning until one side is lovely and browned, then turn over to brown the other side. Set aside in a casserole dish.

Reduce the heat to medium and add the bacon to the pan. Fry until crisped up, about 8–10 minutes. Transfer to the dish with the pork. Add the butter to the same pan and cook the onion, leek and garlic, stirring, for about 10 minutes until everything is soft. Stir in the apple, sage and mixed herbs, and cook for another minute. Add the stock, bay leaf, mustard, cornflour mixture, pepper and salt. Stir to combine. Carefully pour into the casserole dish and muddle everything around.

Cover with a sheet of baking paper, then the lid. Bake in the preheated oven for 2½ hours, or until the meat is tender. Remove from the oven and season to taste with salt and pepper.

Increase the oven temperature to 200°C fan-bake.

Put the kumara in a pot of salted, cold water and place over a medium-high heat. Simmer for 15–20 minutes, until tender. Drain well. Return the kumara to the pot over a low heat for a minute or so to evaporate any excess moisture. Add the butter and mash. Season to taste with salt and pepper.

Spoon the pork mixture into a large baking dish and spread the mash on top (or just use the casserole dish if you prefer). Toss the breadcrumbs in the olive oil and scatter over top.

Bake in the oven for around 20 minutes, or until golden on top and bubbling. Serve with salad or your favourite steamed greens.

1kg boneless pork shoulder

neutral oil, e.g. grapeseed, for frying

200g bacon, chopped

50g butter

1 large onion, chopped

1 leek, chopped

8 cloves garlic, peeled and roughly chopped

2 apples, peeled and thickly sliced

15 fresh sage leaves

½ cup fresh herbs (marjoram, thyme, rosemary, fennel, parsley, oregano)

1 cup chicken stock

1 fresh bay leaf (or 2 dried)

2 tbsp Dijon mustard

1½ tbsp cornflour mixed with ¼ cup stock or water

1 tsp finely ground black pepper

1 tsp salt

Topping

1kg kumara, peeled and chopped

50g butter

½ cup breadcrumbs

2 tbsp olive oil

Sausagey Kumara Bake

2 x 400g cans chopped tomatoes
(Italian are good)

1 tbsp tomato paste

1 tbsp brown sugar

¼ cup chopped fresh parsley,
plus extra to serve

2 tsp balsamic vinegar

1½ tsp dried oregano

1 tbsp fresh thyme leaves

1 tsp chopped fresh rosemary
(optional)

1 tsp salt

½ tsp finely ground black pepper

6–8 good-quality sausages

1–2 medium orange kumara,
peeled and chopped

½ cup Kalamata or Sicilian olives

1 punnet cherry tomatoes

½ cup finely grated Parmesan
(optional)

PREP 5 MINUTES **COOK** 45 MINUTES **SERVES** 4–6

Quick, simple and very tasty — this may become a regular on the weekly rotation. The sausages look wrinkly here because that's just what happens when you take sausages out of the oven. Embrace the wrinkly deliciousness!

Preheat the oven to 180°C regular bake.

In a large baking dish, combine the chopped tomatoes, tomato paste, brown sugar, parsley, vinegar, oregano, thyme, rosemary (if using), salt and pepper. Add the raw sausages to the dish.

Toss the kumara in a bowl with a little olive oil and press in around the sausages.

Dot the olives around and scatter the cherry tomatoes over. Season everything again with salt and pepper.

Bake in the preheated oven for 45 minutes.

Scatter with Parmesan (if using) and parsley, and serve.

Curried Sausages

6–8 sausages

50g butter (or 3 tbsp neutral oil, e.g. grapeseed or coconut)

2 onions, chopped

2 carrots, chopped

1 large apple, finely chopped (I leave the skin on)

5 cloves garlic, crushed or chopped

1 tbsp finely chopped or grated fresh ginger

2 tsp mild curry powder

2 tsp garam masala

2 tsp ground turmeric

½ tsp finely ground white or black pepper

½–1 tsp chilli powder (optional)

1 x 400ml can coconut milk

1½ cups chicken stock

½ cup water

3 tbsp fruit chutney

1 tbsp tomato paste

1 cup frozen peas (or 2 cups chopped spinach)

1 tbsp lemon juice

chopped coriander or parsley, to serve

Chelsea's tips

♥ If you like it spicy, you can either use a hot curry powder or add a pinch of chilli flakes or the chilli powder.

PREP 15 MINUTES **COOK** 1 HOUR **SERVES** 4–6

I don't try to be hip or cool when I write my recipes. I'm not influenced by anything other than what tastes and feels good, and what I think you guys will like. Food is not fashion! And that's why you're looking at a recipe for sausage curry right now. It's not glamorous but, by George, it's delicious — and, I think, a pretty great way to use sausages. It's also a lovely mild curry that, hopefully, the whole family will enjoy. A few harmless veges are hidden in there, too, for good measure.

Pour a splash of oil into a large frying pan over a medium heat. Cook the sausages in the pan until browned all over (they don't have to be cooked through). Set aside until cool enough to handle, then slice into 1cm pieces.

Add the butter or oil to the same pan over a medium heat, along with the onion and carrot. Cook, stirring, for 10 minutes until the onion is sticky, soft and golden. Stir in the apple, garlic and ginger and cook for another 2 minutes. Add the spices and cook for another minute, stirring. If it looks a little dry you can add a tablespoon of the coconut milk.

Transfer the sausages to the pan along with the coconut milk, stock, water, chutney and tomato paste, stir to combine and leave to simmer over a medium-low heat for around 30–40 minutes. Give it a stir every now and then.

Add the frozen peas or spinach and cook for a further 5 minutes. Stir through the lemon juice and season to taste with salt — you may need more than you think.

Scatter with coriander or parsley. Serve with rice or mash, and slaw or vegetables.

Chorizo & Egg Pie

3–4 pre-rolled sheets flaky puff
  pastry
extra virgin olive oil
6 uncooked chorizo sausages
4 large onions, sliced
3 cloves garlic, crushed
2 tsp paprika
½ tsp chilli powder
⅓ cup finely chopped parsley
1 tbsp lemon juice
1½ tsp salt
1 tsp finely ground black pepper
1 cup grated Edam or Colby
  cheese
10 free-range eggs
handful cherry or grape
  tomatoes, or a few sliced ripe
  tomatoes (optional)
1 free-range egg whisked with
  1 tbsp milk (egg wash)
sesame or poppy seeds for
  sprinkling (optional)

Chelsea's tips

♥ If you can be bothered rolling
  out 2 x 400g blocks of pastry, I
  find it puffs up better (if you're
  concerned about presentation).

PREP 35 MINUTES **COOK** 1 HOUR **SERVES** 6–8

Chorizo sausages have the lovely Spanish flavours of paprika and garlic,
so they make a nice twist on a classic sausage and egg pie — it's a flavour
match made in heaven. The onions are cooked until they are just starting
to caramelise which adds a luscious flavour of its own.

Preheat the oven to 180°C fan-bake and set a rack in the lower half of the
oven. Grease a 25cm baking or pie dish (metal is best for a crispy base).

Line the base and sides of the dish with pastry and prick base with a fork
(patch pastry pieces together with water if you need to). Keep some pastry
for the lid.

Heat a splash of the extra virgin olive oil in a large frying pan over a
medium-high heat. Add the sausages and cook until browned all over (they
don't have to be completely cooked through). Set aside on a chopping
board to cool a bit.

Add ¼ cup of olive oil and the onion to the same pan along with a pinch of
salt. Cook, stirring every now and then, for about 10 minutes until golden
and browned — some darker brown bits are okay. Add the garlic, paprika
and chilli and cook for another couple of minutes.

Remove from the heat and stir through the parsley, lemon juice, salt and
pepper.

Slice the sausages into small pieces and combine with the onion. Stir in the
cheese.

Break half the eggs into the base of the pie. Pour the sausage mixture on
top and muddle it all around with your fingers so it combines a little. Break
the remaining eggs on top and muddle it again. Place the tomatoes on
top (if using). Season with a little salt and pepper again.

Cover with a pastry lid, pressing down firmly all around the edges to seal.

Brush the pastry all over with the egg wash, and poke a couple of steam
holes in the top. Sprinkle with sesame or poppy seeds if you like.

Bake in the lower half of the oven for 1 hour. Remove from the oven and
leave to cool for 15 minutes or so before slicing.

Serve warm or cold.

Scotch Eggs

5 free-range eggs, unshelled

6–8 beef sausages

3 tbsp finely chopped parsley

½ tsp salt

½ tsp finely ground black pepper

⅓ cup plain flour

1–2 free-range eggs, lightly
  beaten

1½ cups breadcrumbs

2 tbsp extra virgin olive oil

2 cups neutral oil, e.g.
  grapeseed, for shallow-frying

———

Chelsea's tips

♥ The eggs will peel more easily
  if they are not too fresh, so this
  recipe is a good way to use up
  older eggs. Save your fresh ones
  for poachies!

PREP 10 MINUTES **COOK** 15 MINUTES **SERVES** 5

I know these are totally old school, but I just think they're such a fabulous, economical way to make a delicious meal packed with protein and goodness. I remember making Scotch Eggs in home economics when I was 13, and thinking it was the best thing I had ever eaten. I did try baking these as an option, but the result was a bit 'meh' and I decided if you're going to make them, you might as well make them properly and that means shallow-frying. Golden, crispy, delicious! Yum cold from the fridge, too.

Place the eggs in a saucepan of cold salted water. Place over a high heat, cover with a lid and bring the eggs to the boil. As soon as they are boiling, remove the lid, reduce the heat to medium and start a timer for 2 minutes.

Immediately drain the eggs, and run them under cold water until cool — a couple of minutes.

Slice the skins of the sausages open and squeeze out the meat into a bowl. Add the parsley, salt and pepper. Scrunch with clean hands to combine.

Carefully peel the eggs. Divide the sausage mixture into 5 portions and wrap up the eggs — take a portion, flatten it out thinly in your hand, and place the egg on top. Then close the meat around the egg. Shape it in your cupped hands until it forms an even layer that encloses the egg. Repeat with the remaining eggs.

Put the flour in a small bowl, the beaten eggs in a medium bowl and the crumbs in another medium-large bowl. Add the olive oil to the crumbs and mix to combine.

Dust each sausage ball in flour, then coat evenly with the egg, letting the excess drip off. Lastly, coat each ball in the crumb.

Heat the frying oil in a medium saucepan (it should go about 5cm up the sides). Place over a medium heat and leave until hot — about 180–190°C if you have a thermometer.

When the oil is hot, fry the balls in batches for about 6 minutes, turning to brown all over. Set aside on a wire rack over paper towels to drain.

Serve hot, warm or cold with ketchup (see page 164) and either veges or a salad. Great picnic fodder!

Singapore Fantasy Noodles

500g boneless pork belly slices

2 cups chicken stock

peanut, avocado or grapeseed
  oil, for frying

1 tsp sesame oil

2 shallots (or 1 medium onion),
  finely chopped

7 cloves garlic, chopped

1 red chilli, finely chopped (or
  ½ tsp chilli flakes)

3 free-range eggs, lightly beaten

400–500g fresh hokkien noodles/
  thin egg noodles

200–300g raw prawns, shelled
  (thawed if frozen)

2 tbsp fish sauce

2 tsp soy sauce

½ cup finely chopped chives,
  parsley or coriander

¾ tsp finely ground black pepper

juice of 1 lime

———

Chelsea's tips

♥ Look for pork belly slices
  in the meat section of your
  supermarket. They may also
  be called pork strips.

PREP 35 MINUTES **COOK** 20 MINUTES **SERVES** 6

The name I've given this recipe is so bad, it's good! It's my version of the Singaporean street-food dish, Hokkien Mee. I first tried it in Singapore when I was lucky enough to explore the incredible food markets there. It tastes a million bucks, which usually surprises people because it certainly doesn't look very glam, but the amount of flavour hiding in that humble exterior is rather impressive. Pork belly slices all the way, baby.

Arrange the pork belly slices in a layer on the bottom of a medium saucepan. Pour in the stock — you can add a little water to cover the meat if necessary. Cover with a lid, place over a medium-low heat and bring to a gentle simmer for about 30 minutes, or until the meat is tender. Transfer the pork strips to a chopping board to cool slightly. Pour the stock into a jug to use later.

When the pork is cool, remove and discard the very top layer of skin — leave the fat there as it adds a wonderful flavour to the dish. Chop the meat into small pieces.

In a large frying pan or wok, heat 2 tablespoons of the frying oil over a high heat. Add the pork pieces and stir-fry until browned and crispy. Set aside, leaving the frying oil in the wok.

Turn the heat down to medium. Add the sesame oil, shallots or onion, garlic and chilli, and stir-fry for a few minutes until golden. Turn up the heat to high, carefully pour in the egg, and use a wooden spoon to scramble it.

Add the noodles and pork to the pan, and stir-fry for a couple of minutes so everything is coated in the cooking oil.

Add 1½–2 cups of the reserved stock and simmer rapidly for 5–10 minutes, until you only have a little bit of liquid left.

Stir through the prawns, fish sauce, soy sauce, herbs and pepper. Cook for another couple of minutes until the prawns are cooked through.

Serve in bowls with the lime juice squeezed over the top, and extra salt and pepper if you like.

One-pan Spanish Prawn & Chorizo Rice

2 cups medium-grain rice

500g raw prawn cutlets

extra virgin olive oil

200g cured Spanish chorizo sausage, sliced (not the fresh ones that need cooking)

2 brown onions, roughly chopped

2 stalks celery, finely chopped

1 red onion, halved and sliced

8 cloves garlic, roughly chopped

1 tbsp paprika

1 tsp smoked paprika

big pinch chilli flakes

2 cups chicken stock

1 x 400g can cherry tomatoes, drained (or use 1 punnet fresh if in season)

1 lemon, halved

2–3 spring onions, chopped

½ cup finely chopped parsley

——

PREP 15 MINUTES   **COOK** 30 MINUTES PLUS 10 MINUTES RESTING TIME
SERVES 8

Another godsend of the one-pan wonders. This is easy, relatively quick to prepare and so delicious you might almost feel a bit guilty you didn't really put much time and effort into it. In other words, totally ideal! If your poor old box of paprika has been sitting open in the pantry for a year, it's worth grabbing a fresh supply for this recipe, as it's the star of the show.

Rinse the rice in a sieve for 30 seconds, or until the water runs clear. Set aside in the sieve over a bowl for at least 15 minutes to drain.

If the prawns are frozen, defrost them in a bowl of warm water, then drain and set aside. You can remove the tails if you like.

For this dish, you need a big frying pan that has a lid. If you don't have a lid, you can just fudge it with 2 layers of foil — so get those ready to fit your pan.

Place your frying pan over a medium-high heat. When hot, add 1 tablespoon extra virgin olive oil and fry the chorizo briefly until golden brown. Transfer to a bowl and set aside.

Reduce the heat under the pan to medium and add ⅓ cup extra virgin olive oil (you need more than you think, trust me). Stir in the brown onion and celery, and cook, stirring often, for 10–15 minutes until everything is soft and turning golden and sticky.

Add the red onion and garlic and cook for another 5 minutes.

Stir through the paprikas and chilli and cook for another minute.

Add the well-drained rice to the pan and turn the heat to high. Stir-fry everything for a few minutes until the rice is nice and hot and popping. Pour in the stock and cherry tomatoes, stir well and bring to the boil. As soon as it reaches a boil, reduce the heat to very low and cover tightly with the lid — you only want the very minimum of steam escaping. Leave it at the gentlest simmer for 20 minutes.

Remove the lid and scatter the prawns and chorizo on top of the rice, then replace the lid. Cook for 5 minutes, then turn off the heat and leave to stand for another 10 minutes.

Give it a stir with a wooden spoon. Season to taste with salt and pepper. Squeeze the lemon over and stir through the spring onions and parsley.

Goes well with a simple green salad or steamed veges.

Crunchy Ham & Cheese Croquettes

125g butter

¾ cup plain flour

500ml full-fat milk

200g chopped champagne ham
(or 80g dried serrano ham/
prosciutto)

1 cup grated cheddar cheese

¼ cup finely chopped parsley

1¼ tsp salt

½ tsp finely ground white pepper

¼ tsp finely ground black pepper

neutral oil, e.g. grapeseed, for
frying

Coating

½ cup plain flour

2–3 free-range eggs, lightly
beaten

2 cups dried breadcrumbs

Chelsea's tips

♥ Test if the oil is hot enough by
adding a 5cm piece of bread
to it. If the bread sizzles and
turns golden brown in about
10 seconds, it is hot enough.

♥ Always take care when deep-
frying. Gently place the food in
the oil to prevent hot splashes.
Don't overcrowd the saucepan —
this will slow down the cooking.
If the oil starts smoking, it is too
hot. Turn the heat off and have
a metal pot lid or tray handy to
cover the saucepan if it catches
fire.

PREP 10 MINUTES PLUS 5+ HOURS CHILLING TIME **COOK** 15 MINUTES
SERVES 4 AS A LIGHT MEAL

The Spanish do a mean ham and cheese croquette — crisp and golden
on the outside, melty and oozy in the middle. Forgive me while I place-
drop again, but I tried these at an incredible food-market in Spain, where
vendors were selling all the Spanish delicacies under the sun. I became
over-excited when I found the croquettes — they looked so tasty all lined
up there. Next thing you know, as soon as I've ordered and paid, he
shoves them in the microwave on a paper plate! Soggy sacrilege! So, I can
tell you with certainty that my version will be *better* than the 'real thing' in
that case.

Line a 20cm x 15cm (or near enough) tray or dish with baking paper.

Place the butter in a medium-large saucepan over a medium heat. When
foamy, add the flour and stir for a minute or so. Remove the pan from the
heat and slowly pour in the milk, whisking constantly, until smooth.

Add the ham and replace the saucepan over a medium heat. Stir
continuously with a wooden spoon for about 5 minutes, until the mixture is
very thick and gluggy. Stir through the cheese, parsley, salt and peppers.

Tip the mixture into the prepared tray or dish, cover and refrigerate for at
least 5 hours until firm enough to slice (it will still be a touch messy), or until
you are ready for it.

Slice the mixture into chunks — roughly 3cm x 7cm, but don't be too picky.
Lightly moisten your hands with cold water and roll each chunk into a
sausage-like shape.

Place the flour, eggs and breadcrumbs in three separate shallow bowls.
Dip each croquette in flour, dust off the excess, then dip in the egg. Let the
excess drain off, then add to the bowl of crumbs and toss to coat well. Set
aside on a tray.

Now dip them all in the egg again and the crumbs again, so they are
double coated — they don't need another flour dip, though.

When all the croquettes are coated, set a medium saucepan with 5cm of
the oil in it over a medium heat. When the oil is hot, about 190°C, carefully
place a few croquettes in (see Chelsea's tips) and cook until dark golden
brown all over — a few minutes. You may want to turn them over a couple
of times to cook them evenly. Remove with a slotted spoon and set aside
on a wire rack to cool slightly. Repeat with remaining croquettes.

Serve hot as a finger food with or without aïoli, ketchup (see page 164) or
mayo. Or serve as a main with a salad or veges, and potatoes.

Once fried, the croquettes can be cooled completely and then frozen for
up to 3 months. Just reheat them in a 150°C oven for 20 minutes or so, or
until crispy and gooey again.

The Best Lamb Chops

⅓ cup unsweetened yoghurt

⅓ cup extra virgin olive oil

4 stalks rosemary, leaves pulled off and finely chopped

6 cloves garlic, crushed

1 tbsp Dijon mustard

1 tsp finely ground black pepper

2–3 anchovies, finely chopped

1–1.5kg lamb shoulder chops

1 tbsp neutral oil, e.g. grapeseed, for frying

——

Chelsea's tips

♥ These chops are awesome cooked on the BBQ in summer.

PREP 10 MINUTES PLUS 6+ HOURS MARINATING TIME
COOK 10 MINUTES **SERVES** 4–5

Homely old lamb shoulder chops might not be the 'cool' kids on the block, but I love them and, man, do they pack some flavour! Sometimes the shoulder meat can be a little chewy, so this marinade is what you need — the yoghurt helps to tenderise the lamb beautifully, even when cooked more than medium-rare. The overall flavour is amazing — fragrant, zingy and full of garlicky punch. If you like, you can also use lamb loin chops for this recipe.

Combine the yoghurt, olive oil, rosemary leaves, garlic, mustard, pepper and anchovies in a small mixing bowl.

Pat the lamb dry with paper towels. Place in a large resealable bag or large shallow dish. Add the marinade ingredients and toss to coat evenly. Leave to marinate for 6 hours or overnight — or two nights.

Remove the lamb from the fridge 30 minutes before cooking. Season the marinated lamb on both sides with salt — don't forget this bit or it'll lack flavour.

Preheat a large frying pan over a medium-high heat. When hot, add the neutral oil and the lamb chops. Cook for a few minutes on one side until browned and crispy, then turn over and cook the other side for another few minutes. Set aside on a board or in a small roasting tray to rest for 5–10 minutes before serving.

Goes well with simple sides such as sliced tomatoes and lettuce leaves — the Kumara & Caramelised Onion Mash on page 136 is a lovely option, too.

BBQ Butterflied Lamb Leg

1 butterflied lamb leg (about 1.5kg)

Marinade

¾ cup unsweetened yoghurt

¼ cup extra virgin olive oil

1½ tbsp lemon juice

7 cloves garlic, crushed

2 tbsp chopped fresh ginger

2 tsp ground cumin

2 tsp ground coriander

2 tsp ground cardamom

2 tsp paprika

1½ tsp ground ginger

1 tsp ground allspice

1 tsp caraway seeds (optional)

2 tsp ground turmeric

1 tsp finely ground black pepper

1 tsp finely ground white pepper

1 tsp chilli powder

Mint yoghurt drizzle

¾ cup unsweetened yoghurt

1 tbsp lemon juice

1 bunch fresh mint, leaves finely chopped

1 clove garlic, crushed

———

PREP 10 MINUTES PLUS 6+ HOURS MARINATING TIME
COOK 20 MINUTES **SERVES** 6–8

This is a nice, easy way to feed a crowd of people in summer — add a selection of salads and sides, some wraps or pitas, and you're away. The yoghurt marinade helps tenderise the meat — you can leave it in the fridge for one or two nights. Just make sure you take it out of the fridge a good hour or two before you cook it, so the lamb isn't chilled when it goes on the BBQ.

Place the marinade ingredients in a bowl and stir to combine.

Remove the lamb from its packaging and pat dry all over with paper towels. Have a large resealable bag or a large bowl ready. Place the lamb and the marinade in the bag or bowl and squish it around with your hands so the lamb is evenly coated. Cover and refrigerate for at least 6 hours — overnight or even 2 nights is best.

Remove the lamb from the fridge 1–2 hours before cooking. Season generously all over with salt.

Preheat a clean BBQ grill to a medium-high heat. Brush the grill with oil. When it's preheated, drizzle the lamb on both sides with oil to coat evenly, then place on the grill. Leave for a minute or so until seared, then turn over and sear the other side.

Now turn the grill down to medium-low and leave the lamb sitting there for about 7 minutes. The bottom should be golden and crisp up nicely without being a charred mess. Turn the lamb over and cook the other side for another 7 minutes.

The cooking times are really a guide only — it varies depending on your BBQ, the size of the lamb leg and how chilled the meat is when you put it on. When it's medium-rare, the meat should still be soft when you prod it, but with some springiness and resistance. Rare lamb will just feel totally soft and squidgy. I don't recommend cooking it any more than medium-rare — medium at the most. Try to resist the urge to slice into the lamb to check it, because precious juices will run out. Just use the prod test — the more you cook, the better you'll get at figuring it out.

Rest the lamb, loosely covered with foil, on a wooden board for at least 15 minutes before slicing.

To make the yoghurt drizzle, combine all the ingredients in a small bowl.

Season the lamb again with salt and pepper and serve with the yoghurt drizzle. Accompany with salads and bread.

Lamb & Rosemary Cannelloni

neutral oil, e.g. grapeseed, for frying

500g lamb mince

¼ cup extra virgin olive oil

1 onion, finely chopped

4 cloves garlic, crushed

1½ tbsp very finely chopped fresh rosemary leaves

2 x 400g cans chopped tomatoes (use Italian-style if you like)

1 cup chicken stock

1 cup grated pumpkin or kumara

1 cup chopped spinach (leaves only)

1 tbsp tomato paste

2 tsp brown sugar

1 tsp salt

¼ tsp cayenne pepper (or pinch chilli flakes)

⅓ cup fresh mint leaves, roughly chopped

250g dried cannelloni tubes

200g crème fraîche

1½ cups grated cheese (mozzarella, cheddar or a mixture)

———

Chelsea's tips

♥ If you can't find dried cannelloni tubes, you can use dried lasagne sheets and assemble it a little like a lasagne, with just layers of mince and pasta — then the cheeses on top.

♥ Leftover cannelloni will keep in the fridge for a good few days or in the freezer for up to 3 months.

PREP 20 MINUTES   **COOK** 45 MINUTES   **SERVES** 4–6

This is a recipe that's been on my website for years and people kept asking me what book it's in. It wasn't in one, so I thought I'd better do something about that! I have, however, made a few tweaks to make it even more delicious — I couldn't help myself. While cannelloni takes a bit of fiddling to get the stuffing in, it's totally worth it and there's something really satisfying about the whole process. And it tastes amazing!

Preheat the oven to 180°C regular bake.

Heat a dash of frying oil in a large saucepan over a high heat. Once hot, add the lamb, breaking up any lumps with a wooden spoon. Leave to sizzle until browned, then stir to brown the rest. Set aside in a bowl.

Reduce the heat to medium and add the olive oil and onion to the same pan. Cook for about 7 minutes, stirring occasionally, until the onion is soft. Stir in the garlic and rosemary and cook for another minute.

Add the tomatoes, stock, pumpkin or kumara, spinach, tomato paste, sugar, salt and cayenne pepper or chilli flakes. Simmer for about 10 minutes or until thickened into a sauce — a little bit of juice is needed as the pasta tubes will absorb it.

Stir through the mint, then spoon enough sauce out of the pan to cover the base of a 20cm x 30cm baking dish.

Add the lamb mince to the remaining sauce in the pan, and simmer for another few minutes. Season to taste with salt and pepper.

Now, to stuff the cannelloni tubes. The easiest way is to wait for the meat sauce to cool down and use your fingers. Or, while hot, use a butter knife to shove the sauce into the tubes. As the tubes are filled, place them in the baking dish on top of the sauce. Keep going until you run out of sauce or tubes — any extra sauce can be poured over top of the cannelloni in the dish.

Spread the crème fraîche over the cannelloni to cover them as best you can, then sprinkle with the cheese and season with salt and pepper. Cover with foil and bake in the preheated oven for 40 minutes. If you like, you can grill the top uncovered for a few minutes so it's bubbling.

Let sit for 10 minutes then serve with veges or a fresh green salad.

Lamb, Beetroot & Kumara Salad with Feta Cream

PREP 20 MINUTES **COOK** 1 HOUR 15 MINUTES **SERVES** 5–6

2 medium beetroot, unpeeled

3 stalks rosemary, leaves pulled off and chopped

4 medium kumara, peeled

3 red onions, cut into wedges

2 whole bulbs garlic, unseparated and unpeeled

¼ cup extra virgin olive oil, plus extra for drizzling

4 lamb rumps, skin and fat removed

neutral oil, e.g. grapeseed or coconut, for frying

250g green beans, topped

lemon wedges

¼ cup chopped fresh mint, parsley, coriander or chives

Feta cream

100g feta, crumbled

1 cup unsweetened yoghurt (I like Greek)

2 tbsp finely chopped mint leaves

1 tbsp Dijon mustard

2 tsp honey

1 tsp lemon juice

———

Chelsea's tips

♥ If you have any bread lying around, tear into pieces and fry in ¼ cup extra virgin olive oil until golden and crisp. Use these as croutons to garnish.

There are some delicious flavours and textures going on here! This salad works equally well in winter or summer as it's quite grunty, and you can serve it warm or cold. You can also use lamb steaks for this — you don't need to oven-bake them, just fry until rare to medium-rare. Leftover roast lamb would also be amazing. Pumpkin could be used instead of kumara.

Preheat the oven to 180°C fan-bake.

Cut the top and tails off the beetroot, then slice in half. Place on a large square of foil, drizzle with olive oil, sprinkle with salt and pepper, and stuff a bit of the rosemary in between the halves. Close up the foil.

Cut the kumara into 4cm pieces. Place in a large roasting tray along with the onion, garlic bulbs, remaining rosemary and the olive oil. Season well with salt and pepper, and toss to combine. Add the beetroot parcels to the tray and bake in the preheated oven for an hour. Remove from the oven and set aside.

Increase the oven to 220°C fan-bake.

Remove the lamb from the fridge 30 minutes before cooking. Pat dry with paper towels and season generously all over with salt and pepper.

Heat a frying pan over a high heat. When very hot, add 1 tablespoon frying oil and the lamb, and fry to brown all over. Transfer to a roasting tray and roast in the oven for 10 minutes for medium-rare. Remove from the oven, cover lightly with foil and rest for at least 10 minutes.

To make the feta cream, combine the feta, yoghurt, mint, mustard, honey and lemon juice in a bowl. Add half the roasted garlic by squeezing it out of the skin. Stir to combine and season to taste with salt and pepper.

To cook the beans, rinse the frying pan and add ⅓ cup water, then replace over a high heat. When boiling, add the beans and cook for a few minutes, turning the beans every now and then, until bright green and cooked but still firm to the bite. Plunge into a bowl of cold water if you like, to keep them nice and green.

Place the beans in a large salad bowl with the kumara, onion and remaining squeezed-out garlic.

Remove the beetroot from the foil when cool enough to handle, discard the rosemary and rub the skins off. Slice finely. Just before serving, add to the salad and toss through.

Slice the lamb and arrange on the salad. Drizzle with a little extra virgin olive oil, squeeze over some lemon juice, and season with salt and pepper. Scatter over the chopped fresh herbs. You can dollop with the feta cream — and have extra on the table so people can help themselves.

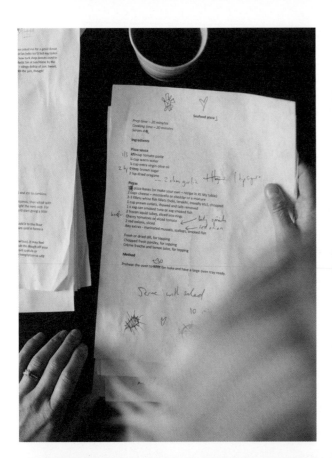

Speedy Soy Salmon Parcels

¼ cup soy sauce

¼ cup hoisin sauce

1½ tbsp rice wine vinegar (or
    1 tbsp apple cider vinegar)

1 tbsp honey

1 tbsp finely grated ginger

1 tbsp sweet chilli sauce

zest of 1 lemon, plus 1 tsp juice

zest and juice of 1 orange

½ tsp Chinese five-spice

4 star anise (optional)

½ tsp black pepper

600–700g salmon fillets

fresh chopped coriander or
    parsley

1 red chilli, chopped and
    deseeded (optional)

——

PREP 10 MINUTES **COOK** 12 MINUTES **SERVES** 4

This is a such a neat way to whip up a quick, tasty dinner in record time. People will love their individual portions of fish, and the tasty sticky sauce left is just the best for drizzling over the rice. It's not hard to do at all and the little parcels help keep the fish nice and moist.

Preheat the oven to 200°C regular bake.

Place the soy sauce, hoisin sauce, vinegar, honey, ginger, sweet chilli sauce, lemon zest and juice, orange zest and juice, five-spice, star anise (if using) and pepper in a small saucepan. Simmer over a medium heat for a few minutes until reduced and thickened slightly.

De-bone the salmon if it needs it, using fish tweezers or kitchen tweezers. The skin can stay on, or take it off if you like. If they are huge pieces, you can cut them in half.

Cut a 40cm length of baking paper for each salmon piece you have. You can also use foil, but I prefer the paper — I feel it's better for the flavour, and for you.

Place a piece of salmon on one side of the paper and spoon sauce on top of it (make sure you get a whole star anise in each one, if using star anise).

Fold up the paper a bit like you would a present, then fold up the edges and press the creases tightly so the parcel holds in place. Arrange the parcels side by side in a roasting tray.

Bake in the preheated oven for about 10–12 minutes.

Unwrap carefully, scatter with the fresh herbs and chilli (if using) and serve on rice. Pour the extra liquid from the paper over the salmon and rice, too.

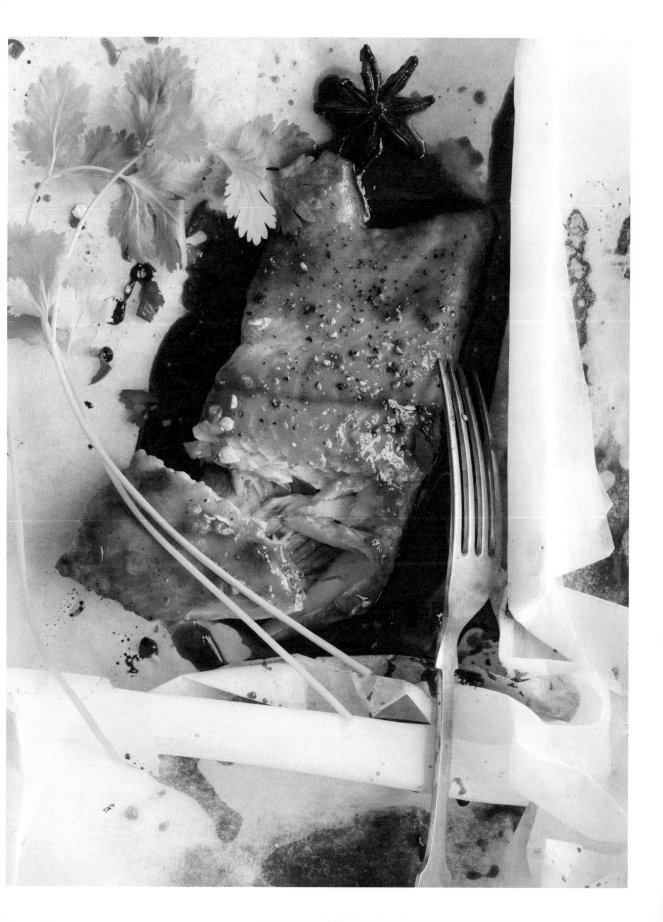

Thai Prawn Fritters with Dipping Sauce

Mandy's Asian dipping sauce

½ cup sweet chilli sauce

1 tbsp fish sauce

1 tsp sesame oil

2 cloves garlic, crushed

2 tbsp soy sauce

2 tbsp brown sugar

zest and juice of 2 limes (or 1 lemon)

Fritters

⅔ cup frozen peas

800g uncooked prawn cutlets, tails removed

⅓ cup finely chopped fresh coriander

1 free-range egg, lightly beaten

1 free-range egg white, lightly beaten

¼ cup finely chopped shallot or red onion

2 tsp fish sauce

1½ tsp cornflour

1 tsp lime juice

½ tsp finely ground white pepper

½ tsp ground cumin

½ tsp salt

pinch chilli flakes

neutral oil, e.g. grapeseed, for frying

PREP 10 MINUTES   **COOK** 15 MINUTES
SERVES 4 (MAKES ABOUT 16 SMALL FRITTERS)

These fritters are light and bursting with fresh flavours. It's a really nice way to use frozen prawns, too. If you like, you can substitute the prawns with chopped fresh fish. Thanks to Mandy Scott for sharing the amazing dipping sauce recipe — it's a star in its own right, really!

Place the sauce ingredients together in a small bowl and whisk to combine. Set aside for the flavours to infuse.

Thaw the peas in a jug of hot water, then drain.

Place the prawns and peas in a food processor and pulse until you have a chunky mixture. You don't want a paste, but you want the mixture to be broken down enough for it to hold together nicely. A mixture of chunkier bits and some mushy bits is fine. If you don't have a food processor, you can very finely chop/mince some of the prawns.

Transfer the prawn mixture to a large mixing bowl. Add the coriander, egg and egg white, shallot or onion, fish sauce, cornflour, lime juice, pepper, cumin, salt and chilli flakes. Add a good crack of black pepper and stir well with a fork to combine evenly.

Heat a little oil in a frying pan over a medium-high heat. When the pan is hot, add ¼ cup portions of the mixture to the pan and fry for 1–2 minutes until browned on one side. Turn with a metal fish slice and cook the other side. Set aside on a wire rack to cool.

Serve hot with the dipping sauce on the side. Goes well with the Asian Slaw on page 150.

Seafood Pizza

PREP 20 MINUTES **COOK** 10 MINUTES PER PIZZA **SERVES** 6

I've just finished stuffing my face with this pizza as I write, and I honestly think it was one of the nicest homemade pizzas I've eaten. Not exactly 'traditional' — but still a solid 10 out of 10, Mike and I both agreed. Don't turn your nose up at the anchovies in the pizza sauce — you won't even notice they are there but they add an amazing depth of flavour. And the canned smoked salmon might seem a bit strange too, but it works. You can add or swap out any seafood you like — marinated mussels, scallops, smoked fish.

Preheat the oven to 240°C fan-bake and place a large oven tray (or pizza stone) inside so it preheats in the oven.

To make the pizza sauce, whisk all the ingredients together in a medium mixing bowl until combined.

To assemble the pizzas, divide the sauce among the bases and smooth out almost to the edges with the back of a spoon. Scatter with grated cheese, then salmon or tuna and spinach. Top with the seafood, tomato, onion and fennel seeds. Season with salt and pepper.

Carefully transfer each pizza to the preheated oven tray (or pizza stone) and bake in the preheated oven for about 10 minutes, or until bubbling and just turning golden. Remove from the oven and transfer to a chopping board. Cook the remaining pizzas.

While the pizzas are cooking, combine the crème fraîche with a squeeze of lemon juice, and season with salt and pepper. Stir to combine.

Squeeze lemon juice over the pizzas and drizzle with the crème fraîche. Sprinkle with fresh herbs. Slice into quarters and serve with a very simple green salad.

Pizza sauce

⅓ cup tomato paste

¼ cup warm water

¼ cup extra virgin olive oil

2 tsp dried oregano or dill tips

2 cloves garlic, crushed

2 anchovies, minced

½ tsp salt

Pizzas

3 large storebought pizza bases (or make your own — see the recipe in *At My Table* and at chelseawinter.co.nz)

2 cups grated cheddar or mozzarella cheese

1 x 200g can salmon or tuna with a natural smoked flavour, drained

1 cup finely chopped spinach

2 white fish fillets (hoki, tarakihi, snapper, trevally), chopped

1 cup defrosted prawn cutlets, tails removed if wished

2 frozen squid tubes, defrosted and sliced into rings

handful cherry tomatoes or 1 chopped tomato

1 large red onion, sliced

2 tbsp fennel seeds

To serve

⅓ cup crème fraîche

lemon wedges

¼ cup chopped fresh parsley (or 2 tbsp fresh dill)

Salmon Quiche

2 sheets savoury short pastry (or
  1 x 400g block, rolled out)

75g butter

1 onion, finely sliced

1 leek, finely sliced

½ tsp salt

1½ cups chopped spinach

1 tbsp lemon juice

6 free-range eggs

300ml cream

zest of 1 lemon

1½ tsp dried dill (or 1½ tbsp fresh
  chopped)

1 tsp salt

½ tsp finely ground white pepper

1 cup grated cheddar cheese

200g hot-smoked salmon

——

Chelsea's tips

♥ If you are using a ceramic dish,
you will need to blind bake the
pastry case first to prevent it
going soggy. Place a piece of
foil or baking paper inside the
dish so it covers the pastry base
and sides. Fill two-thirds full with
baking beads, uncooked rice or
lentils. Bake in a 180°C fan-bake
oven for 10 minutes, then remove
the beads and foil or paper,
and bake for another 6 minutes.
Remove from the oven and cool.
Fill and bake as usual.

PREP 25 MINUTES **COOK** 30 MINUTES **SERVES** 6–8

DELICIOUSNESS! This quiche is a good way to make a little bit of salmon
go the extra mile. There's no blind baking involved, which makes it easy
to prepare — but in order to avoid the dreaded soggy bottom, it's best
to use a shallow metal baking dish. These are inexpensive and you can
usually get them at a supermarket or any homeware store. If you don't
have one, I've included tips for blind baking below.

Preheat the oven 200°C fan-bake and set a rack in the lower half of the
oven.

Grease the base and sides of a shallow metal baking or roasting dish
(about 28–30cm diagonally from corner to corner). If you don't have one,
use a springform cake tin — line the bottom with baking paper and grease
the sides. Or you can use a quiche tin.

Line the dish with pastry. Use one sheet for the base, then cut the
remaining sheet up for the sides, joining the seams at the base with a little
water and pressure. Make sure there are no cracks — patch them up with
extra pastry if you need to.

Put the butter in a frying pan over a medium heat. When foamy, add the
onion, leek and first measure of salt, and cook, stirring, for 10 minutes until
very soft and starting to caramelise. Add the spinach and lemon juice. Stir
for a minute until the spinach wilts, then remove from the heat. Allow to
cool to warm.

Break the eggs into a large mixing bowl with the cream, lemon zest, dill,
second measure of salt and pepper. Whisk until smooth.

Tip two-thirds of the cooled veges into the base of the pastry case. Add
one-third of the cheese, then chunks of salmon. Top with another third
of cheese, then pour the cream mixture over the top. Scatter with the
remaining cooled veges and cheese.

Place the dish in the oven and set a timer for 5 minutes. After 5 minutes,
turn the heat down to 160°C fan-bake. Cook for a further 25–30 minutes. It
should be lightly golden and puffy, and slightly wobbly still in the middle.

Serve warm or cold with a squeeze of lemon juice and a crisp fresh salad
with vinaigrette. Can be frozen for up to 3 months.

Fish with Herb Sauce & Crispy Capers

¼ cup capers, drained

neutral oil, e.g. grapeseed, for frying the capers

800g white fish fillets (snapper or tarakihi)

¼ cup plain flour or cornflour

Sauce

50g butter, plus extra for frying

1 clove garlic, crushed

zest of 1 lemon

1½ tbsp lemon juice

⅓ cup finely chopped fresh soft herbs (parsley, dill, thyme, chives)

——

PREP 15 MINUTES **COOK** 15 MINUTES **SERVES** 4–5

When you have beautiful fresh fish, it's tempting to cook it with nothing but a bit of butter and lemon. Sometimes, though, it's nice to do something a little fancier — and if you're entertaining, this recipe is perfect. The fish is still the star of the show, but I've added a few lovely fresh flavours to take it from an everyday dish to something special. As always, it's quick and easy to prepare — just don't overcook the fish! This goes perfectly with a fresh green salad, or green beans in winter.

Drain the capers on a paper towel to get any excess moisture off.

Heat 2cm of the neutral oil in a very small saucepan over a medium-high heat. Add the drained capers and fry for a few minutes until the capers puff up and open out. Remove with a slotted spoon and drain on paper towels.

To make the sauce, melt the butter in a small frying pan over a medium-low heat and add the garlic. Cook gently for 5 minutes or so, but don't brown the garlic. Add the lemon zest and juice, stir and set aside off the heat.

Pat the fish fillets dry with paper towels. Season with salt and pepper, then dust with flour or cornflour (you can dredge it on a plate or shake in a bag). Shake off the excess.

Place 25g butter in a large frying pan over a medium-high heat. When the pan is hot and the butter foams, place a few fish fillets in the pan. Turn them over when the underside is deep golden, then cook on the other side for a minute or so — you actually want the fish to be just undercooked when you take it out of the pan (it will finish cooking out of the pan).

Rest the fish, lightly covered with foil, on a warm plate while you cook the remaining fillets (add more butter to the pan as needed).

When you're ready to serve, add the fresh herbs to the lemony butter and mix to combine, then taste and season with salt and pepper if need be.

Serve the fish with the herb sauce drizzled over the top and sprinkled with some fried capers. It's lovely with a fresh salad and the Crunchy Potato Wedges on page 138.

Mum's Smoked Fish Pie

PREP 25 MINUTES **COOK** 35 MINUTES **SERVES** 6

500–600g smoked fish
100g butter
2 onions, chopped
2 carrots, finely chopped
4 cloves garlic, crushed
2 tbsp plain flour
1⅓ cups milk
1 cup cream
2–3 cups chopped spinach
1 tbsp grated horseradish
1 tbsp Dijon mustard
zest of 1 lemon
2 tbsp lemon juice
1 tsp finely ground white or black
    pepper
1½ tsp salt
⅛ tsp cayenne pepper
½ cup chopped fresh herbs
    (parsley, dill, chives, fennel),
    plus extra to serve

Topping

1kg Agria potatoes, scrubbed
50g butter
¼ cup cream
¾ cup grated cheese
2–3 slices good-quality bread
3 tbsp extra virgin olive oil

——

This recipe is one of my favourites! I watched Mum make smoked fish pie last summer at Great Barrier (with a kahawai I had caught, I might add!). When I got home, I embellished it with a few of my own flourishes. Those of you with my first book, *At My Table*, will know there's already a smoked fish pie recipe in there; however, this version is much quicker to prepare. It's so lovely and creamy, I think your whole family will love it.

Remove the skin, bones and brown flesh from the smoked fish, leaving the flesh in chunks as big as possible. Set aside.

Place the butter in a large frying pan over a medium heat. Add the onion and carrot and cook, stirring, for 10 minutes until soft. Stir through the garlic and cook for another minute.

Add the flour and cook, stirring, for a couple of minutes. Remove the pan from the heat and add the milk in a steady stream, stirring all the time. When all the milk is incorporated, place back over a medium heat. Add the cream. Let it simmer for 10 minutes or so until reduced and thickened.

Place the fish pieces, spinach, horseradish, mustard, lemon zest and juice, pepper, salt and cayenne in the sauce, and stir gently to combine. You want to keep the fish pieces as chunky as possible for texture. Leave to simmer for 5 minutes. Stir through the herbs and pour into a baking dish.

Preheat the oven to 180°C fan-bake.

Put the potatoes in a saucepan of salted water, place over a medium-high heat and simmer until tender — about 20 minutes. Drain well, then return to the pan with the butter and cream. Mash very roughly, skins and all. Season to taste with salt and pepper.

Spoon the potatoes over the fish mixture and sprinkle with the cheese.

Process or chop the bread to a chunky crumb. Toss with the olive oil and sprinkle on top of the cheese.

Bake in the preheated oven for 35 minutes until bubbling and golden (you can grill the top at the very end if you like). Scatter with herbs and serve with steamed greens or a salad.

Thai BBQ Whole Snapper

PREP 10 MINUTES **COOK** 20 MINUTES **SERVES** 4–5

2–3 whole fish (e.g. snapper or tarakihi), gutted

sea salt

2 limes, thinly sliced, plus extra to serve

1 lemon, thinly sliced

big handful fresh herbs (coriander, mint, basil, chopped lemongrass), plus extra to serve if wished

1–2 red chillies, chopped

¼ cup finely sliced ginger

neutral oil, e.g. grapeseed, for brushing the fish

Mandy's Asian dipping sauce (see page 84) or fish sauce, to serve (optional)

Chelsea's tips

♥ If you've caught your own fish, you'll need to scale it (consult Google for the method that suits you best). If you're going to a fishmonger, they will do it for you. When you're choosing a fish, look for clear, bright eyes — not cloudy, dull and sunken. The fish should smell fresh and salty like the sea, and the body should feel firm and springy. When you get it home, put it in the fridge (or a chillybin), sitting on and covered with ice, for up to 24 hours.

♥ Make sure your BBQ grill is scrupulously clean — oil it then scrub it with a wire brush, or a couple of balls of wadded-up foil. If it's not clean, the fish will stick.

Cooking fish this way may seem daunting, but I've made it so everyone with a BBQ can do it. Either get a couple of nice whole fish from the fishmonger, or if you've got loads of freshly caught fish, this is a great change from the ol' fillets cooked in butter. It's a bit more fiddly to eat, but not everything in life needs to be quick and easy. Just enjoy the moment sharing a beautiful gift from the sea with some good people.

Remove the fish from the fridge about an hour before you plan to cook it so it's not going on the BBQ chilled.

Place the fish on a chopping board and pat dry inside and out with paper towels.

Using your sharpest knife, make a series of cuts right down to the bone along each side of each fish. The cuts should be about 5cm apart (this helps the fish cook evenly). Sprinkle some salt on each side of the fish and rub it into the cuts.

Sprinkle a good amount of salt in the belly cavity, then stuff it with lime, lemon, herbs, chilli and ginger. Use toothpicks or skewers to seal the cavity shut and stop everything falling out.

Brush both sides of the fish with oil to prevent it sticking to the BBQ.

Preheat your very clean BBQ grill to a medium-high heat. When the grill is nice and hot and just before you put the fish on, oil it.

Carefully place the fish on the grill. Resist the temptation to touch it for about 10 minutes (for a medium fish). At first, the skin will stick to the grill horribly — but as it cooks, it will mostly unstick itself as it crisps up.

When it's time to turn, use a couple of large metal turners or fish slices to first shimmy the fish off the grill (some of the skin will always want to stick — just get it off as cleanly as you can) and then turn the fish over. If it's a big fish, you could get someone to help. Leave the other side to cook for another 10 minutes. The total cooking time depends on how big your fish is and how hot your BBQ is — you be the judge. When all the flesh is white/opaque, it's cooked.

Very carefully transfer to a platter or plate, squeeze with lime juice and scatter with extra herbs if you like, and let people help themselves. The sauce on page 84 or fish sauce is delicious drizzled on top, if you can be bothered.

You can eat the crispy skin (it's delicious). Use forks to pluck the flesh from the bones (be careful of the small ones, though). Have side plates ready for people to discard any bones or scales they find.

Perfect served with the Asian Slaw on page 150 and BBQ Pizza Bread on page 152.

Cheesy Pumpkin, Bacon & Cauliflower Bake

1.5kg pumpkin (or butternut or orange kumara), peeled and chopped into 3cm pieces

extra virgin olive oil

250g bacon, rind removed, chopped

2 large onions, roughly chopped

8 cloves garlic, roughly chopped

2 stalks rosemary, leaves finely chopped

2 tsp dried oregano

pinch chilli flakes

1 head cauliflower, chopped into small florets

1 cup fresh breadcrumbs (or ½ cup dried)

Sauce

75g butter

⅓ cup plain flour

2 cups warm milk

2 cups grated Edam, Colby or mild cheese

———

Chelsea's tips

♥ You can make this dish meat-free simply by omitting the bacon, and it will still be delicious.

♥ Add a cup of frozen peas before baking for extra greens.

PREP 30 MINUTES **COOK** 35–40 MINUTES **SERVES** 4–6

Do you feel you need to get more veges into your family? Well, this is how you do it. It might not look like much on paper, but right here is a seriously delicious vegetable dish. You're looking at an awesome concoction of roasted pumpkin, caramelised onion, cauliflower, bacon and herbs bound in a cheese sauce — all baked with a crispy crumb topping. SOLD!

Preheat the oven to 180°C fan-bake (190°C regular bake) and grease a 30cm x 20cm baking dish.

Place the pumpkin pieces on a roasting tray and drizzle generously with extra virgin olive oil. Season with salt and pepper and toss to coat evenly. Bake in the preheated oven for 20 minutes until almost cooked through (it will finish cooking later).

While the pumpkin is cooking, add 2 teaspoons of the olive oil to a large frying pan over a medium heat. Add the bacon and onion and cook, stirring, for about 15 minutes until the bacon and onion are golden and turning a bit sticky. Stir in the garlic, rosemary, oregano and chilli flakes and cook for another minute. Add the cauliflower and cook for 10 minutes until it starts to soften. Season with salt and pepper to taste (the bacon is already salty, so don't go too crazy). Remove from the heat.

To make the sauce, place the butter in a medium saucepan over a medium-low heat. When melted, add the flour and cook, stirring, for a few minutes until pale but not browned. Remove from the heat and slowly pour in the milk, whisking all the time to prevent lumps. Replace over the heat, stir in three-quarters of the cheese and season to taste with salt and pepper.

Combine the sauce and roasted pumpkin with the bacon mixture, then pour into the baking dish. Sprinkle the remaining cheese over top.

Toss the breadcrumbs in a bowl with 2 tablespoons of the olive oil and a pinch of salt, and sprinkle on top of the cheese.

Bake, uncovered, in the oven for 35–40 minutes, or until golden and bubbling and the cauliflower is tender. Serve with steamed seasonal greens or a salad.

Meat-free Burgers

Patties

3 tbsp olive oil

2 large onions, **finely** chopped

4 cloves garlic, crushed

500g Portobello **mushrooms, finely** chopped

1 tsp Vegemite or Marmite

1 x 400g tin black beans, drained and roughly mashed

¼ cup dried breadcrumbs

¼ cup rolled oats

½ cup finely grated Parmesan

2 free-range eggs, lightly beaten

1 tbsp tomato paste

2 tbsp chopped fresh parsley

1 tsp Worcestershire sauce

1 tsp salt

¾ tsp finely ground black pepper

To serve

6 buns, buttered

fillings (lettuce, red onion, gherkins, avocado, beetroot and/or sliced cheese)

condiments (mayo, pesto, hot English mustard, tomato sauce and/or relish)

Chelsea's tips

♥ It might take a little effort to chop the mushrooms and onions finely, but it will help the patties hold together better than if they were in big chunks.

PREP 40 MINUTES PLUS 1 HOUR CHILLING TIME **COOK** 10 MINUTES
SERVES 4–6

With this recipe, I wanted to create something that the whole family would actually enjoy on meat-free Monday. Well, the feedback I had about the patties really took me by surprise. Everyone LOVED them, Mike even announced he preferred them to normal meat patties — whoa. So, this one could be a bit of a favourite, I reckon. Here's an idea — why don't you sneakily try them out on your family without telling them they're meat-free? I wonder if they'd even notice . . .

Heat the olive oil in a frying pan over a medium-low heat, add the onion and cook, stirring, for 10–15 minutes until soft and golden. Add the garlic and cook for another minute.

Add the mushrooms and Vegemite or Marmite, turn the heat up to medium-high, and continue to cook. The mushrooms will eventually lose moisture and shrink down. Keep stirring for about 10 minutes, or until most of the moisture has evaporated (you don't want a soggy mixture). It should start to go mushy. Transfer to a large mixing bowl and leave to cool for 20 minutes or so.

Place the black beans, breadcrumbs, oats, Parmesan, eggs, tomato paste, parsley, Worcestershire sauce, salt and pepper in the bowl with the mushrooms. Scrunch to combine using clean hands.

Shape into six patties, cover and refrigerate for at least an hour, or until you need them (overnight is fine).

To cook, heat a frying pan (or BBQ grill) over a medium-high heat. Add a little oil and fry for a few minutes each side until cooked through.

Serve on toasted buttered burger buns with your choice of fillings and condiments.

Roasted Tomato Pasta

1.5kg very ripe tomatoes

1 onion, chopped

2 whole bulbs garlic, unseparated
   and unpeeled

⅓ cup extra virgin olive oil

1 tbsp brown sugar

1 tbsp balsamic vinegar

1½ tbsp fresh oregano leaves (or
   2 tsp dried)

1 tbsp chopped fresh rosemary or
   thyme leaves

1½ tsp salt

To serve

pasta cooked to *al dente*

basil leaves

freshly grated Parmesan

———

Chelsea's tips

♥ If you're not a fan of tomato
skins, you can either pick them
out before serving or remove
them beforehand — slice an X in
the bottom of each tomato and
sit in a bowl of just-boiled water
for 5 minutes. Drain, and pull the
skins off. Personally, though, I
don't mind them in there.

PREP 5 MINUTES   **COOK** 1 HOUR 30 MINUTES
MAKES ENOUGH FOR 6–8 SERVINGS OF PASTA

In late summer when there are loads of lovely cheap ripe tomatoes
around, this is such a beautiful way to serve them. Bung it all in the oven
where it will caramelise and all those beautiful flavours will develop, then
mush it up a bit, stir it through hot cooked pasta, freshen it up with basil
and seasonings, and, bam, you'll be transported to Italy!

Preheat the oven to 160°C regular bake.

Halve the tomatoes, then cut out the firm white cores and tops and
discard. Place in a large roasting tray with the remaining ingredients and
toss gently to combine. Arrange everything in an even layer and bake in
the preheated oven for 1 hour 30 minutes. It should look very mushy and
caramelised — pop it back in the oven for another 15–20 minutes if you
think it needs it.

Let cool slightly, then transfer to a bowl. Squeeze the roasted garlic out of
its skin into the bowl and discard the skin.

Mush it around to break it up into more of a sauce, and season to taste
with salt and pepper.

To serve, stir through hot cooked pasta with an extra slurp of olive oil.
Sprinkle with torn basil leaves and freshly grated Parmesan.

Leftover sauce keeps in an airtight container in the fridge for a few days.

Falafel

1 cup dried chickpeas

1 cup frozen broad beans, defrosted (available in the freezer section of your supermarket)

1 cup chopped fresh coriander (leaves and stalks)

¾ cup chopped fresh parsley

2 cloves garlic

3 spring onions, chopped

1 tbsp lemon juice

1½ tsp salt

1½ tsp ground cumin

1 tsp ground turmeric

1 tsp ground coriander

½ tsp finely ground black or white pepper

¼ tsp ground cinnamon

¼ tsp ground ginger

¼ tsp ground allspice

¼ tsp chilli powder (optional)

sesame seeds (optional)

neutral oil, e.g. grapeseed, for frying

Chelsea's tips

♥ For extra flavour, try rolling the falafel in sesame seeds before frying.

PREP 15 MINUTES PLUS 1+ HOUR CHILLING TIME (PLUS SOAKING OVERNIGHT FOR CHICKPEAS) **COOK** 15 MINUTES **SERVES** 4

This is a surprisingly easy and extremely delicious vegetarian (and vegan) dish, bursting with the tasty flavours of the Middle East. It might seem tempting to use canned chickpeas, but the end result won't be as nice. Hunt down some dried ones; they make for light, crispy falafel perfection. These are lovely as a meal with some pitas or flatbreads, hummus, cucumber, yoghurt and tabbouleh (see chelseawinter.co.nz for the recipes).

To soak the chickpeas, place them in a bowl with double the amount of cold water, cover and set aside overnight. After this they still probably won't feel soft, because they are raw. This is fine! Drain off the liquid.

Put the chickpeas in a food processor with the defrosted broad beans, and all the remaining ingredients except the sesame seeds (if using) and oil. Process until you have a pretty smooth paste — you'll need to scrape down the sides with a spatula quite a few times to get it all incorporated. Taste it and add more salt, pepper or lemon juice if you think it needs it.

Transfer to a non-metallic bowl, cover and refrigerate for at least 1 hour, or until you're ready to fry them.

Shape the mixture into little mini-patties about 5cm across.

Add oil 5cm deep to a medium saucepan over a medium-high heat. If you have a cooking thermometer, it should be about 180°C.

Fry the falafel in batches so you don't crowd the pan — about 2 minutes each side. They will go a little on the dark side rather than golden. As long as they aren't black that's fine, it's just the nature of the filling.

Halfway through if you think you need to add more oil to the pan, do so, but let it come back up to temperature before frying more falafels.

Set aside to drain on a wire rack sitting on paper towels.

Eat the falafel as soon as you can after frying them. Serve with warmed pitas, wraps or flatbreads along with hummus, ribboned cucumber, yoghurt (or coconut yoghurt) and mint.

Easy Roasted Pumpkin Soup

PREP 10 MINUTES **COOK** 1 HOUR 15 MINUTES **SERVES** 4–6

2.5–3kg pumpkin
50g butter
5 cloves garlic, roughly chopped
1 onion, peeled and halved
olive oil for drizzling
4 cups chicken or vegetable stock
⅔ cup cream (plus extra for
serving)
¼ tsp finely ground black pepper
¼ tsp finely ground white pepper
squeeze of lemon juice (optional)
pesto (see page 160 or
storebought), to serve
¼ cup fresh chopped parsley, to
serve

———

Chelsea's tips

♥ If you have some fresh thyme
leaves, add them to the pumpkin
cavities while cooking.

I say 'easy' because with this recipe you don't have to experience the emotional trauma and anguish associated with peeling a whole raw pumpkin. That's gotta be a win! It's a very simple recipe with just a few ingredients that make a luscious, creamy, satisfying soup bursting with fresh pumpkin flavour. Everyone who has tried this soup has absolutely raved about it.

Preheat the oven to 190°C fan-bake.

Cut the pumpkin in half whichever way feels easiest for you. Some people swear by microwaving the whole pumpkin for a minute before cutting it. Just keep your fingers well clear of that knife when you are applying downward pressure!

On the rounded base of each pumpkin half, cut a little slice off so it has a flat little bum to sit on in the oven. Scrape the seeds out with a spoon and discard.

Place the pumpkin halves flesh-side up in a roasting tray. Divide the butter and garlic between the two pumpkin cavities. Season well with salt and pepper, and cover the tops with foil.

Drizzle each onion half in olive oil and wrap in foil. Add to the tray.

Roast in the preheated oven for 1 hour, or until the pumpkin is tender. When cool enough to handle, tip the melted butter into a large saucepan and use a large spoon to scrape the pumpkin flesh out of the skins — discard the empty skins. Add the pumpkin flesh and onion halves to the saucepan.

Pour the stock into the saucepan, place over a medium heat, cover and simmer for about 10–15 minutes.

Add the cream and peppers. Transfer the saucepan carefully to a board on the bench, and use a hand-held stick blender to purée the soup until it's very smooth and velvety. If you don't have a stick blender, you can let the soup cool to warm, then use a food processor or blender — but don't do this while the soup is hot.

Pour the soup back into the saucepan and taste it. Season with more salt until you are happy with the taste. A squeeze of lemon can be nice, too.

Serve in bowls with extra cream and pesto (see page 160) or chopped fresh parsley and buttered toast.

Leftover soup will keep in the fridge until the cream's use-by date or in the freezer for up to 3 months.

slow

As winter slowly grasps us in its chilly grip, it seems like a good idea to slow things down a little bit. Short days, cosy living rooms, early dinners, love-worn slippers, and maybe a golden crackling fire if you're lucky (which sadly, I'm not — can I come to your place?). Quite possibly the most delicious thing about the frosty season, though, is the food that goes along with it: soul food, slow food, food for sharing. And how good is it heading into a long, cold evening knowing you've had dinner bubbling away in the background all day, just quietly doing its thing? Those beautiful savoury aromas meandering around the house, coaxing hungry troops to crowd around the kitchen table, stomachs aglow. The recipes in this section are comforting, nourishing and meltingly tender. They are designed to warm the very cockles of your hearts. Enjoy!

Beef Cheeks in Red Wine

Beef

1kg beef cheeks

neutral oil, e.g. avocado or
grapeseed, for frying

500ml red wine

50g butter

2 tbsp extra virgin olive oil

1 leek, chopped (or 1 large onion)

1 large carrot, chopped

2 stalks celery, chopped

400g button mushrooms

2 stalks rosemary

2 anchovies, chopped

1 tbsp balsamic vinegar

1 tbsp brown sugar

2 bay leaves

1 tbsp cornflour mixed with
2 tbsp water

25g butter

chopped fresh parsley, to serve
(optional)

———

PREP 40 MINUTES **COOK** 4 HOURS **SERVES** 4–6

Beef cheeks are such an awesome cut, and it's a good feeling to know you're using different parts of the beast — it's given its life for us, after all. Cooked long and slow they are superbly tender with loads of flavour. Ask your butcher if you can't find them — they'll be able to get them in for you. This is also lovely served sprinkled with the gremolata from the Osso Buco recipe on page 120.

Preheat the oven to 130°C regular bake.

Trim any excess fat or sinew from the beef cheeks using a sharp knife and discard. Pat the beef dry with paper towels and season all over with salt and pepper.

Heat a frying pan over a high heat (or use a stovetop-safe casserole dish for this whole process if you have one). When hot, add 1 tablespoon frying oil and then brown the meat (in batches if need be). The meat should end up a nice deep brown all over. Set aside in a casserole dish.

Add ½ cup of the red wine to the pan to deglaze it (this gets all the caramelised meat juices off the bottom, which is where the flavour is). Let the wine bubble up and then pour over the meat.

Replace the pan over a medium heat, add the 50g butter and olive oil along with the leek, carrot, celery and mushrooms. Cook, stirring, for 10 minutes until soft. Add to the casserole dish with the meat, along with the remaining wine, rosemary, anchovies, vinegar, sugar and bay leaves. Mix everything up.

Cover with the lid and bake in the preheated oven for about 4 hours, or until the meat is very tender and pulls apart easily. Remove the meat carefully. Pull into serving-size chunks and set aside.

Strain the cooking liquid through a sieve or colander, set the mushrooms aside and discard the other veges.

Transfer the liquid to a saucepan along with the mushrooms and cornflour mixture. Boil until thickened. Stir through the 25g butter and season.

To serve, add the chunks of beef to the sauce and serve on mash. Scatter with chopped fresh parsley if you like.

Sticky Pork & Crackling Buns

PREP 15 MINUTES **COOK** 3 HOURS **SERVES** 6

1–1.5kg boneless pork belly

1½ tbsp cornflour mixed with
2–3 tbsp water

Braising sauce

4 shallots, roughly chopped (or
2 onions)

1 orange, sliced

1 cup chicken stock (reduced-salt
if you can find it)

1¼ cups soy sauce

1½ cups water

1 cup brown sugar

⅓ cup apple cider vinegar

¼ cup roughly chopped ginger
(skin-on is fine)

¼ cup fish sauce

4 whole star anise

1 tbsp sesame oil

1 tsp Chinese five-spice

¼ tsp chilli flakes

Pickled cucumber (optional)

100ml white wine vinegar

100ml water

50g sugar

pinch salt

1 cucumber, sliced into ribbons

To serve

12 par-baked white buffet rolls

pickled cucumber (see above) or
thinly sliced fresh cucumber

fresh coriander

sesame seeds (optional)

chopped fresh chilli (optional)

———

Chelsea's tips

♥ If you find the sauce is too thick
later when it has cooled, simply
heat it up again with a little water
added.

You are in for a real treat here! The contrasting textures of the tender pork, soft rolls, sticky sauce and the crunchy crackling are just sublime. If you're entertaining, you're going to look very flash indeed — it feels a bit like restaurant food, a feast fit for a king but it's so easy.

Preheat the oven to 220°C regular bake.

Place the shallots and orange slices in the bottom of a deep roasting or baking dish that's not too much bigger than the pork belly.

Pat the pork skin dry with paper towels. If not already scored, use a sharp knife to score slices 1cm apart through the skin and just into the fat (not into the meat). Place in the dish on top of the oranges and shallots.

Place the remaining sauce ingredients in a medium saucepan. Cover and bring to the boil, then carefully pour over the pork belly. The skin will pucker up a bit. Most of the meat should be submerged, but the skin should just be clear of the liquid. This will be the crackling. Wipe the top of the pork belly to dry it off a bit before it goes in the oven. Sprinkle the skin with salt and drizzle with a little olive oil.

Bake uncovered in the oven for 30 minutes. Reduce the temperature to 120°C regular bake and continue to cook uncovered for a further 2½ hours.

If making the pickled cucumber, whisk the vinegar, water, sugar and salt together until dissolved. Add ribbons of cucumber and leave for 15–30 minutes. Drain and cover until needed.

Remove the pork from the oven. Transfer to a roasting tray. Change the oven setting to grill on medium and place the pork back in the oven. Grill until the crackling is puffed up all over — keep a close eye on it so it doesn't burn. Set aside.

Increase the oven temperature to 200°C regular bake.

Strain the cooking liquid through a sieve and add 1½ cups of it to a medium saucepan. Stir through the cornflour mixture. Stir and simmer over a medium heat for 5–10 minutes, until thickened into a nice sauce.

Carefully peel the crackling off the pork belly and chop up into small pieces. Chop the pork into small pieces, and toss in ¼ cup of the sauce.

Arrange the buns on a large tray and cover with a tea towel that's been completely wet then loosely wrung out (this will help steam the buns). Bake in the centre of the oven for about 10 minutes until the rolls are hot, soft and slightly sticky. (Watch closely, as the tea towel will almost be dry shortly after 10 minutes, and do not attempt this in a gas oven.)

Serve the pork, crackling, sauce, pickled or freshly sliced cucumber and coriander in bowls on the table along with the buns and people can make their own. Sprinkle with sesame seeds and chopped fresh chilli if you like.

Rich Beef Goulash

1kg chuck steak (or gravy beef, cross-cut blade or shin)

neutral oil, e.g. avocado or grapeseed, for frying

75g butter (or ½ cup extra virgin olive oil)

2 large onions, finely sliced

1 tsp caraway seeds (optional)

1 green capsicum, sliced

1 red capsicum, finely sliced

400g mushrooms, sliced (optional)

1 cup chicken stock or water

1 stalk celery, whole

3 tbsp paprika (best quality you can find)

1 tbsp plain flour mixed with 3 tbsp water or stock

½ tsp finely ground black pepper

2 tsp apple cider vinegar or lemon juice

½ cup chopped fresh parsley

½ cup sour cream, to serve

———

PREP 20 MINUTES   **COOK** 3½ HOURS IN OVEN; 3–4 HOURS ON HIGH OR 6–8 HOURS ON LOW IN SLOW COOKER   **SERVES** 8–10

This is my take on a classic Hungarian dish that's been around in one form or another since medieval times (which must mean it's good). Paprika is the superstar of this dish — if you can, buy the best quality you can afford. It was a bit odd to leave out all my normal stew staples — tomato paste, herbs, garlic — but it just doesn't need them.

If cooking in the oven, preheat the oven to 130°C regular bake.

Leave the beef steaks whole for now. Pat dry with paper towels and season on both sides with salt and pepper. Set aside on a plate.

Heat a frying pan over a high heat (or use a stovetop-safe casserole dish for this whole process if you have one). When very hot, add a splash of the frying oil, then add the beef in batches and sear to brown all over. Set aside.

Reduce the heat to medium and add the butter or olive oil to the same pan. Add the onion, caraway (if using), capsicum and mushroom (if using), and cook for about 10 minutes until soft. Carefully transfer to a casserole dish or slow cooker. Slice the beef into 5–6cm pieces and add to the dish.

Add the chicken stock or water, celery, paprika, flour mixture and pepper. Stir everything to combine. Cover with a lid and bake in the preheated oven for 3½ hours, or until the meat is pull-apart tender. (Or, in a slow cooker, cook on high for 3–4 hours or low for 6–8 hours.) Stir once or twice during the cooking time.

Remove from the oven (or slow cooker). Discard the celery stalk. If the sauce is too runny, you can transfer it to a saucepan and simmer it for 5–10 minutes until it has thickened to your liking.

Stir through the vinegar or lemon juice and most of the parsley. Season with sea salt to taste. Serve with a big dollop of sour cream, a sprinkling of the remaining herbs and cracked pepper, with boiled new potatoes, egg noodles or mash.

Irish Lamb Stew

1kg boneless lamb shoulder or leg

neutral oil, e.g. grapeseed, for frying

2 tbsp fresh thyme leaves

2 bay leaves

75g butter

4 onions, chopped

2 tbsp tomato paste

2 tsp salt

1 tsp finely ground black pepper

¾ cup beef stock

¾ cup chicken or vegetable stock

3–4 carrots, chopped chunkily

700g Agria potatoes, scrubbed and cut into 5cm chunks

½ cup finely chopped fresh parsley

——

PREP 30 MINUTES **COOK** 3 HOURS **SERVES** 5–6

'Stew' is a word that can conjure up awkward vibes with some people (Mike is one of them). But this time I'm not changing the title of the recipe; this is a stew and it's a bloody good one! Put your prejudices aside and MAKE IT! It's deliciously old-fashioned and superbly comforting. And despite comprising relatively simple ingredients, it delivers massive flavour. Probably one of my favourites in this book, actually. If you can find lamb stock, by all means use this in place of the options given. This recipe is dedicated to my beautiful friend Andrea (or Maumau as I like to call her). She likes a bit of Irish stew. Love you Mau!

Remove the lamb from the fridge 30–60 minutes before cooking.

Preheat the oven to 130°C regular bake.

Pat the lamb dry with paper towels, cut into 7cm chunks and season all over with salt and pepper.

Heat a frying pan over a high heat (or use a stovetop-safe casserole dish for this whole process if you have one). When hot, add 1 tablespoon of the oil and half the lamb. Sizzle until browned on one side, then turn over to brown the other side. Set aside in a casserole dish and repeat with the remaining lamb. Add the thyme and bay leaves to the dish.

Reduce the heat under the pan to medium and add the butter and onion. Cook, stirring, for 5 minutes until soft. Add the tomato paste, salt and pepper and stir to combine. Add the stock, turn the heat up and bring to the boil, then carefully pour over the top of the lamb and herbs.

Cover the casserole dish with a lid and bake in the preheated oven for 2 hours. Add the carrots and potatoes, turn the heat up to 150°C, and cook for another hour, or until the veges are tender. Give it a good stir to break up the potatoes a little bit — they will help thicken the sauce.

Before serving, you can choose to spoon off some of the oil on top, if there is any. Remove the bay leaves. Stir through most of the parsley, and season to taste with extra salt and pepper if you think it needs it.

Serve with crusty buttered bread and the remaining parsley. Goes well with some simply steamed broccoli, too.

Leftover stew will keep in an airtight container in the fridge for 1 week or in the freezer for up to 3 months.

Slow-cooker Pork Rib Quesadillas

Pork

1–1.5kg pork ribs

2 onions, roughly chopped

5 cloves garlic, roughly chopped

3 tbsp brown sugar

2 tbsp tomato paste

1 tbsp malt vinegar

2 tbsp paprika

1 tsp ground cumin

1 tsp ground coriander

1 tsp finely ground black pepper

1 tsp chilli powder (optional)

2 cups chicken stock

1 x 400g can chopped tomatoes
   in juice (Mexican-style tinned
   tomatoes work well too)

To assemble

2–3 cups grated cheddar cheese

6–8 wraps or tortillas

1–2 red onions, thinly sliced

1 bunch coriander

⅓ cup jalapeños, chopped

neutral oil, e.g. grapeseed, for
   frying

chipotle or tabasco sauce

sour cream or plain yoghurt

lime wedges

Chelsea's tips

♥ Ensure you have a thin layer of
cheese at the top and bottom of
the filling because it sticks to the
wraps and prevents everything
from falling apart when you turn
it over.

♥ The pork ribs can cook on low in
the slow cooker overnight.

♥ You can cook the pork ribs in the
oven in a covered casserole dish
for 2–3 hours at 150°C regular
bake if you prefer.

PREP 15 MINUTES **COOK** 4–5 HOURS ON HIGH OR 7–9 HOURS ON LOW **SERVES** 4–5

A nice and easy way to use pork ribs, this Mexican-style meat is deliciously tasty and will shred easily by the end. Stuffed in a crispy-fried tortilla shell with melted cheese and a few delicious condiments, these quesadillas make a meal everyone will be happy about! The filling can be made in advance and kept in the fridge — and then the quesadillas can quickly be assembled and fried when you're ready.

If you need to, cut the ribs into two pieces. Place the ribs in the slow cooker, meaty-side down.

Add the onion, garlic, sugar, tomato paste, vinegar, paprika, cumin, coriander, pepper, chilli (if using), chicken stock and tomatoes. If you like, chop the coriander stalks from the bunch of coriander and add. Cover and cook on high for 4–5 hours, or low for 7–9 hours.

When the pork is very tender and can be pulled apart easily, carefully transfer it from the slow cooker to a chopping board.

Sit a colander over a medium saucepan and carefully tip the sauce from the slow cooker into it. Discard the veges.

Place the pan with the cooking liquid over a medium-high heat and simmer rapidly for about 10–15 minutes, or until reduced by about half to a nice sauce consistency.

Shred the pork meat into pieces and place in a bowl — discard the bones and sinew. Stir through the sauce and season with salt and pepper.

To make the quesadillas, sprinkle a good amount of the cheese over one half of a tortilla or wrap. Add some of the pork mixture with a good amount of onion, coriander leaves and a sprinkling of jalapeños. Top with more grated cheese. Season with salt and pepper (a squeeze of lime is nice too). Fold the other side over to make a semi-circle. Squash it down as best you can without everything coming out. The trick is not to put so much filling in that it all falls out when you turn it — a couple of centimetres thick once squashed is about right.

Heat a large frying pan with a dash of oil over a medium-high heat. Add the quesadilla (you might be able to fit two at a time) and fry for a couple of minutes until browned and crispy on one side. Carefully turn over and cook the other side.

To serve, slice the quesadillas into wedges and accompany with the sauces and condiments you like. These are great served with a slaw or salad.

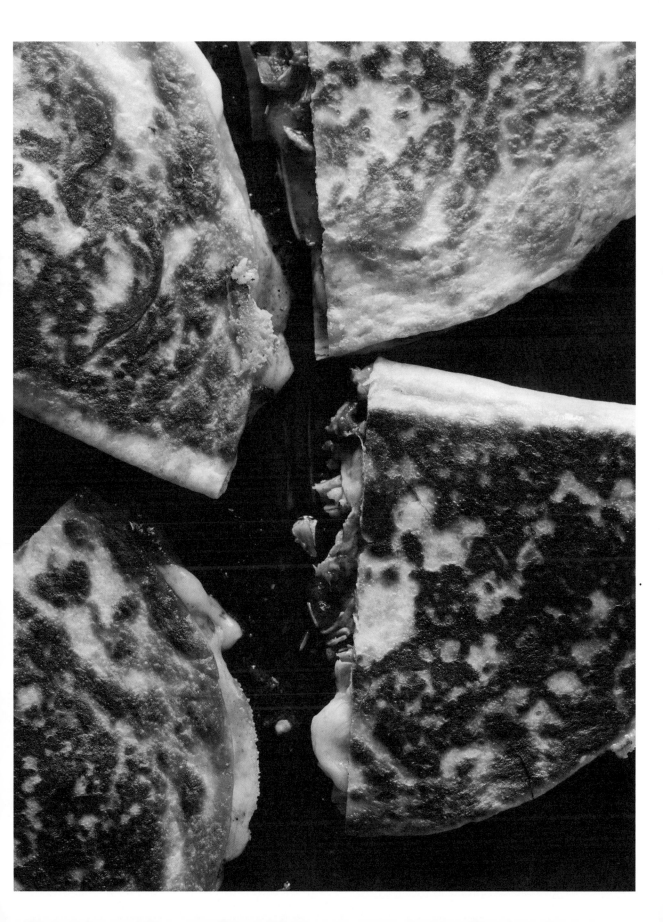

Osso Buco with Gremolata

PREP 25 MINUTES **COOK** 3–4 HOURS **SERVES** 4

4 beef or veal shins on the bone (about 1–1.5kg)

neutral oil, e.g. grapeseed, for frying

1½ cups dry white wine

75g butter (or ¼ cup extra virgin olive oil)

1 onion, finely chopped

2 stalks celery, very finely chopped

6 cloves garlic, roughly chopped

¼ cup packed whole fresh sage leaves

2 tbsp finely chopped fresh rosemary

½ tsp ground allspice

¼ tsp ground cinnamon

2 cups chicken stock

3 dried bay leaves (or 2 fresh)

25g butter

lemon wedges, to serve (optional)

Gremolata

½ cup finely chopped fresh parsley

2 cloves garlic, crushed

2 tsp lemon zest

———

'Osso buco' is Italian for 'bone with a hole'. In the photo you can see the wee holey bones that make up part of a cross-cut veal (young beef) shank. You should be able to find it at most supermarkets and all good butchers. It's quite economical and has a boss flavour — it's also very tough, so needs the low and slow treatment, after which it falls off the bone and melts in the mouth! I've topped this with a fresh gremolata, which brings the flavours of the dish alive. This one was Dad's favourite of all the recipes I tried on him!

Preheat the oven to 130°C regular bake.

Pat the beef or veal dry with paper towels. Using a sharp knife or kitchen scissors, cut through the band of sinewy stuff that goes around the outside edge of the shin — cut in two places. This stops it puckering up in the pan.

Season both sides of the meat generously with salt and pepper. Heat 1 tablespoon of the frying oil in a large frying pan over a high heat. When the pan is very hot, add half the meat and let it sizzle without turning until it's a deep brown on one side. Turn to brown the other side, then set aside in a casserole dish. Repeat with the remaining meat.

Reduce the heat under the pan to medium, and add the wine. Let it bubble up for 30 seconds or so, scraping all the browned bits of meat from the bottom with a wooden spoon. Pour over the meat.

Add the butter (or oil) to the pan and when it foams, add the onion and celery. Cook, stirring, for about 8 minutes until soft and transparent. Add the garlic and cook for another minute. Stir in the sage, rosemary, allspice and cinnamon. Pour in the stock, bring to the boil, then carefully pour or spoon everything into the casserole dish over the meat. Poke in the bay leaves. Stir to cover the meat as best as possible.

Cover the casserole dish with a lid and bake in the oven for 3–4 hours, or until the meat is very tender. Check on it once or twice while it's cooking and rearrange the meat if you need to poke it down under the liquid.

To make the gremolata, combine all the ingredients together, cover and refrigerate until needed.

Once cooked, very carefully remove the meat from the dish and set aside. If necessary, spoon some of the oil off the top and discard.

If you feel the sauce needs thickening, transfer it to a large saucepan or frying pan and boil until thickened up a bit. Stir through the butter. You can choose whether to strain it or not.

Serve the meat on mash (the Creamy Potato & Parsley Smash on page 134 is good), pasta or polenta with lashings of the sauce spooned on top. Sprinkle with gremolata and give it a crack of pepper and a squeeze of lemon if you like.

Melting Lamb with Roasted Garlic Jus

Lamb

2–2.5kg lamb leg, bone-in

2 onions, roughly chopped

3 whole bulbs garlic, unseparated and unpeeled

¼ cup extra virgin olive oil

3 tbsp finely chopped fresh rosemary

zest of 2–3 lemons

4 anchovies, finely minced

Jus

2 tsp cornflour mixed with 2 tbsp water

2 tsp lemon juice

____

PREP 15 MINUTES **COOK** 5½ HOURS **SERVES** 8

Slow-roasting lamb has got to be one of the most sensational aromas you could ever have wafting out of your kitchen. This slow-cooked recipe leaves you with superbly tender meat, bursting with a rich flavour, that almost falls off the bone. It couldn't be easier — the oven does all the hard work, which makes it a no-brainer for entertaining. And that gravy . . .

Remove the lamb leg from the fridge at least an hour before cooking — 2 or 3 hours earlier is fine. Leave it in its wrapper.

Preheat the oven to 120°C regular bake.

Place the onion and garlic bulbs in the bottom of a roasting dish (preferably one with high sides) and toss with a little olive oil, salt and pepper. Set the garlic bulbs to the side of the dish so the lamb doesn't sit on them.

Pat the lamb leg dry all over with paper towels.

Add the olive oil to a small bowl with the rosemary, lemon zest and anchovies. Stir to combine. Rub all over the lamb and season generously with salt and pepper all over. Place the lamb in the roasting dish on top of the onion.

Cover with a lid (or a double layer of foil) and bake in the oven for 5 hours.

Remove the lid, drizzle with a little more oil and cook uncovered for a further 30 minutes. By now, the meat should pull apart fairly easily when you spear a carving fork into it and wiggle it. If not, it might need a little longer at 120°C.

Remove the lamb from the dish, set aside on a warmed plate or tray, lightly cover with foil and leave to rest for 30 minutes before serving.

While the lamb is resting, make the jus. Remove the garlic bulbs from the roasting dish. Drain the cooking liquid through a sieve, then discard the solids and return the liquid to the roasting dish (only if your dish is metal or enamel — if it's ceramic, transfer everything to a medium saucepan instead).

Squeeze the cooked garlic from their skins into the cooking liquid. At this point if it doesn't look like you have a lot of liquid, you can add some extra stock or water. Add the cornflour mixture and lemon juice, stir and place on the stovetop over a medium heat.

Simmer for 5–10 minutes until thickened and reduced slightly — you don't want a thick gravy, just thick enough to coat the meat. Season to taste with salt and pepper.

To serve, pull the meat apart and serve with the gravy. Goes well with the Kumara and Caramelised Onion Mash on page 136.

Fragrant Ginger Beer Pork

1kg pork shoulder, pork strips or boneless belly

neutral oil, e.g. grapeseed, for frying

2 onions, chopped

500g mushrooms, halved or roughly chopped

2 tbsp finely chopped fresh ginger

7 cloves garlic, chopped

2 tsp Chinese five-spice

1 tsp ground coriander

2 whole star anise (optional)

1 cinnamon stick (optional)

½ tsp finely ground black pepper

¼ tsp finely ground white pepper

pinch chilli flakes

500ml ginger beer (or cider or chicken stock)

2 tbsp soy sauce

1 tbsp apple cider vinegar or rice wine vinegar

1 tbsp brown sugar

2 tsp cornflour mixed with 2 tbsp water

Chelsea's tips

♥ Scatter the dish with chopped fresh coriander or chives, if you like.

PREP 30 MINUTES **COOK** 2 HOURS **SERVES** 4–6

What a lovely way to cook pork! The ginger beer adds a nice little warmth and sweetness in this recipe — paired with subtle Asian spices, it's a very tasty dish indeed! It gets gobbled up in record speed here. You can use several cuts of pork — shoulder, belly, strips or even chops. If you don't have any ginger beer, you can use chicken stock.

Preheat the oven to 160°C regular bake.

Slice the pork into 5–6cm chunks and season all over with salt and pepper. You can leave a little fat on for flavour.

Heat 1 tablespoon of the oil in a large frying pan over a medium-high heat (or use a stovetop-safe casserole dish for this whole process if you have one). When very hot, add the pork in batches, leaving to sizzle until golden brown on one side before turning over to brown the other side. Set aside in a casserole dish while you fry the remaining pork.

Reduce the heat to medium, add another tablespoon of oil to the same pan and add the onion. Cook, stirring occasionally, for 5 minutes until golden. Add the mushrooms, ginger and garlic, and cook for another few minutes. Stir in the five-spice, coriander, star anise and cinnamon stick (if using), black and white peppers and chilli. Pour in the ginger beer (or cider or stock), soy sauce, vinegar and brown sugar, and turn the heat to high. Bring to the boil, then turn off the heat.

Pour the mixture over top of the pork in the casserole dish. Add the cornflour mixture and muddle everything in. Cover with a lid and bake in the preheated oven for 1½ hours. Remove the lid, give everything a good stir, and bake uncovered for another 30 minutes.

Remove the meat from the sauce with tongs and set aside. If you need to, you can simmer the sauce on the stovetop in a saucepan until it has reduced enough for your liking.

Serve the pork on rice with a spoonful of sauce, and accompany with steamed green veges.

Slow-cooker Thai Chicken Curry

Paste

¼ cup peanut oil

3 shallots, peeled and halved

1 bunch coriander, stalks and tops separated

1 tbsp chopped fresh ginger

3 cloves garlic

3 large red chillies, seeds scraped out, chopped

2 tsp ground cumin

2 tsp ground coriander

2 tsp ground turmeric

1 tsp sesame oil

½ tsp mild chilli powder

½ tsp finely ground black pepper

1 tbsp shrimp paste (optional)

½ tsp salt

Curry

500ml coconut cream

1–2 stalks fresh lemongrass, bashed (or 2 tbsp lemongrass paste)

3 tbsp fish sauce

2 tbsp brown sugar

zest of 1 lime or a kaffir lime leaf (optional)

1kg boneless chicken thighs (or 1.5kg bone-in)

1–2 tbsp lime juice

chopped roasted peanuts or cashews, to serve (optional)

Chelsea's tips

♥ If you can't find any red chillies, you can use an extra 1–2 teaspoons mild chilli powder.

PREP 15 MINUTES **COOK** 4–5 HOURS ON HIGH; 7–8 HOURS ON LOW
SERVES 6–8

This recipe will make you happy if you like the idea of walking away from a slow cooker and coming home to fragrant, creamy deliciousness! Don't fret looking at the number of ingredients in the homemade paste — it's all just normal stuff you probably have on hand and it's way better than bought paste. I really recommend you use full-fat coconut cream for this, or your sauce might be a bit thin.

Place all the paste ingredients except the coriander tops in a food processor and process until you have a smooth paste, scraping down the sides.

Scrape the paste into a medium saucepan and place over a medium-low heat. Cook, stirring, for about 10 minutes until the paste is thick and fragrant. (At this point, you can cool and refrigerate the paste in a jar or an airtight container for up to a week.)

Add the coconut cream, lemongrass, fish sauce, brown sugar and lime zest or leaf (if using) to the pan with the paste, and stir to combine.

Put the chicken in the slow cooker and pour the coconut sauce mixture on top. Muddle around to combine. Cover and cook for 7–8 hours on low or 4–5 hours on high.

Once cooked, remove the lemongrass stalks and lime leaf (if using). Stir through the lime juice, then taste — add more chilli, fish sauce, sugar or lime juice until the balance of hot, salty, sweet and sour is to your taste.

If you think the sauce is too thin, you can pour it into a saucepan and place over a medium-high heat on the stovetop. Simmer rapidly, uncovered, until you're happy with it. It doesn't need to be super thick as the rice will absorb it.

Serve with jasmine rice and steamed green beans. Scatter with the chopped coriander tops and chopped roasted peanuts or cashews if you like.

Creamy French Chicken & Vegetable Casserole

PREP 30 MINUTES **COOK** 1 HOUR **SERVES** 6

Another one-pot wonder that I think you guys are going to really love! The combination of fragrant French herbs, tender chicken and vegetables all bound in a creamy sauce is such a winner. Indeed, with these ingredients, it's just really hard to go wrong. The leftovers are amazing, too (if you get any)! You can leave the bacon out if you like.

Preheat the oven to 180°C regular bake.

Pat the chicken dry with paper towels and place in a plastic bag with a good amount of salt and pepper. Shake to coat.

Heat a frying pan over a medium-high heat and add 1 tablespoon frying oil and the bacon. Fry until browned and crisp. Set aside in a casserole dish with a lid. Leave the oil and fat in the pan and put back over a medium-high heat. When hot, add the chicken (you'll need to do it in 2–3 batches so you don't overcrowd the pan). Leave the chicken to sizzle until one side is nice and golden brown. Set aside with the bacon and repeat with the remaining chicken.

Tip the oil from the pan and discard. Add the butter to the same pan, along with the leek, carrot, celery and garlic. Cook, stirring, for 10 minutes until softened and reduced in size. It's good to scrape all the browned bits off the bottom of the pan and get them mixed into the veges. Add the mushrooms and cook for another minute.

Stir the herbs, mustard, lemon zest, bay leaves and white pepper into the veges. Transfer everything to the casserole dish with the bacon and chicken, pour the cream mixture over (or stir through the crème fraîche) and cover with a lid. Bake in the preheated oven for 1 hour.

Serve with steamed new potatoes or mash, and sprinkle with chopped fresh parsley.

1kg boneless chicken thighs (or 1.5kg bone-in)

neutral oil, e.g. grapeseed, for frying

200g bacon, rind discarded, chopped

50g butter

1 leek, outer leaves discarded, finely chopped

2 medium carrots, peeled and finely diced

2 stalks celery, finely chopped

8 cloves garlic, roughly chopped

400g mushrooms, roughly chopped

⅓ cup mixed fresh chopped herbs (thyme, rosemary, sage, marjoram)

1½ tbsp Dijon mustard

zest of 1 lemon

2 dried bay leaves (or 1 fresh)

½ tsp finely ground white pepper

1 cup cream mixed with 1 tsp cornflour (or use 200g crème fraîche)

⅓ cup chopped fresh parsley, to serve

——

Lamb, Lentil & Vegetable Soup

Broth

1kg lamb knuckles or shanks

2 onions, chopped

1 leek, chopped

2 carrots, chopped

handful button mushrooms (optional)

handful fresh herbs (thyme, parsley, sage, rosemary, bay leaf)

3 tbsp apple cider vinegar

2 stalks celery, chopped

2 tsp salt

Soup

4 cups chicken stock

2–3 purple kumara, peeled and grated

1 cup whole green lentils, rinsed

2 carrots, chopped

4 stalks celery, chopped

1 leek, chopped

¾ cup finely chopped parsley

———

PREP 15 MINUTES **COOK** BROTH 4–5 HOURS ON STOVETOP OR 6–12 HOURS IN SLOW COOKER; SOUP 45 MINUTES **SERVES** 10

If you think about it, lamb shanks are a perfect base for a soup. They have loads of flavour, the meat falls off the bone with slow cooking and you end up getting more bang for your buck because you're not buying a shank per person. This homemade broth is just brimming with goodness — you can't buy anything like it. Lentils are so good for you and they bulk up the soup and give it texture — and, of course, it's loaded with veg, too. This recipe makes a whole heap, so you can freeze portions to reheat later on.

If using a slow cooker, place the broth ingredients in the slow cooker, nestle it all in tightly and cover with water (6–8 cups). Cover with a lid and cook on low for 10–12 hours, or on high for 6–7 hours. Alternatively, place the broth ingredients in a large pot, cover with water and simmer with the lid on over a very low heat on the stovetop for 4–5 hours. Allow to cool.

Remove the lamb, pick the good meat off and set aside in a bowl. Discard the bones and any gristle.

Pour the broth through a colander into a large soup pot. Mush the cooked veges sitting in the colander around a bit to get the goodness out. Discard the veges.

Add the stock, kumara and lentils to the pot and place over a medium heat. Allow to simmer for about 30 minutes. Add the remaining chopped vegetables and simmer for another 15 minutes until tender. Add the meat and parsley, stir, and season with salt and pepper to taste. You'll probably need more than you think.

Serve the soup with buttered toast. Keeps in an airtight container in the fridge for 1 week or in the freezer for 3 months.

mix + match

Sometimes, steamed veg and boiled spuds on the side is all we can muster the effort for, and that's just fine. However, if you're ever in the mood for something with a little more oomph to spruce up your dinner, let this section be your inspiration. I've concocted a bunch of tasty recipes that you can mix and match as you please to suit your main course — depending on what you've got a hankering for. Obviously, potatoes are one of my favourite things in the world, so there are a couple of humble spud staples here (if you can bear to tear yourself away from the Crispy Roasted Potatoes in *Homemade Happiness* that is). My favourite cabbage dish, which Mum used to make me as a kid, might just change how you feel about this misunderstood (and usually overcooked) vege — and the Mediterranean bulgur wheat salad might sound a bit scary, but I reckon it'll become your summer favourite. Be inspired, try something new and find deliciousness within this collection of easy-to-prepare sides . . .

Creamy Potato & Parsley Smash

1–1.25kg Agria potatoes

1 tsp salt

75g butter, cubed

¼ cup cream

¾ cup finely chopped curly parsley

½ tsp finely ground white or black pepper

——

PREP 5 MINUTES   **COOK** 20 MINUTES   **SERVES** 4–6

Potatoes, in case you can't tell, are one of my favourite foods of all time. This is a true Chelsea-style side — just boil, drain, smash and go! There's no need to peel the spuds and because it's meant to be chunky, you can stress less about lumps in your mash! We eat this a LOT with fresh parsley from the garden and a good smattering of cracked pepper.

Scrub the potatoes (leave the skins on).

Cut evenly into about 5cm pieces. Place in a saucepan, add salt and fill with water to cover. Cover the pan with a lid, set over a medium heat, and simmer until tender — about 20 minutes.

Drain well, then replace over the stove over a low heat, so the excess liquid steams off. Shake them around a few times.

Remove from the heat. Use a wooden spoon to stir in the butter, cream, parsley and pepper. Now sort of jab the spoon around in the pan so you have some mash, some mushy pieces and some big hunks remaining. Season to taste with salt. Keep warm and serve when needed.

Kumara & Caramelised Onion Mash

3 tbsp extra virgin olive oil
3 onions, chopped
½ tsp salt
1kg orange or red kumara
50g butter
¼ cup milk or cream

——

PREP 5 MINUTES **COOK** 20 MINUTES **SERVES** 4–5

I have to give Mike all the credit for this one — one night he cooked me dinner and this most-delicious mash just materialised out of nowhere and blew me away. I mean, kumara mash is damn good just by itself — but when you add in the rich, savoury flavour of the caramelised onion, it's totally sensational!

Place the oil, onion and salt in a frying pan over a medium-low heat. Cook, stirring frequently, for about 15–20 minutes, until the onion is golden and starting to caramelise. Remove from the heat.

While the onion is cooking, peel and chop the kumara into even-sized pieces. Place in a large saucepan of salted water and simmer for 15–20 minutes, until tender (easily pierced with a fork). Drain the kumara well and return to the saucepan.

Add the butter and milk or cream to the hot kumara and mash together (you can also use a food processer to get it super silky smooth). Stir through the caramelised onion, then season to taste with salt and pepper.

Crunchy Potato Wedges

1kg Agria potatoes
⅓ cup extra virgin olive oil
1 tsp salt

———

PREP 5 MINUTES **COOK** 45 MINUTES **SERVES** 4

These wedges are just the ticket when you want a delicious side with the minimum of effort. You don't even need to peel the potatoes! Just make sure you use a floury potato like Agria to ensure they go nice and fluffy on the inside and crunchy on the outside. It seems like a lot of oil, but that's what makes them amazing — and it's a good healthy oil you're using, anyway.

Heat the oven to 190°C fan-bake.

Scrub the potatoes but don't peel them. Dry them with a clean tea towel, then finish drying them with paper towels so the skin is really good and dry.

Slice the potatoes into wedges. Place in a roasting tray with the oil and salt. Toss to combine and arrange so they aren't touching.

Bake the wedges in the oven for 30 minutes without turning them.

After 30 minutes you can gently give them a toss with a metal turner. If it looks like they have soaked up all the oil, add some more.

Return to the oven and increase the temperature to 200°C fan-bake. Cook for a further 10–20 minutes, or until the wedges are browned and crunchy, turning them a couple of times.

Serve immediately with ketchup (see page 164), mayo or aïoli.

Big Roasted Veges

2 kumara, peeled and chopped into 3cm chunks

3 carrots, peeled and chopped into 1cm chunks

2 beetroot, peeled and cut into 2cm chunks

1–2 eggplants, cut into 5–6cm chunks

2 capsicums, sliced into quarters (optional)

3 onions, quartered

3 whole bulbs garlic, unseparated and unpeeled

⅓ cup extra virgin olive oil

3 courgettes, sliced into 1cm pieces

1 bunch asparagus (optional)

To serve

1 tbsp lemon juice

1 tbsp extra virgin olive oil

———

Chelsea's tips

♥ You can add little flavour boosters to this dish if you like, depending on what else you're serving with it. Fresh chopped rosemary or thyme with a Mediterranean-inspired meal — or cumin, nigella or sesame seeds if it has a more Indian or Moroccan vibe. There are no rules, just have a think about what's in your main meal, and use your noggin.

PREP 10 MINUTES **COOK** 40 MINUTES **SERVES** 6

This is a great dish to make any time of year and it goes with everything. Obviously, you can mix and match and swap out the vegetables depending on what you have, what you like and what's in season — there's a nice mixture suggested here though. They all need to be cut into different sizes as they cook at different rates — I reckon it's just easier than adding them to the oven at different times.

Preheat the oven to 200°C fan-bake.

Arrange the vegetables (except the courgettes and asparagus) on your largest roasting tray or dish. Pull the onion quarters apart into layers so they cook through nicely. Add the olive oil, season with salt and toss the veges to combine.

Roast in the oven for 30 minutes, turning once or twice with a metal fish slice while cooking. Add the courgettes and asparagus (if using), and cook another 10 minutes or so.

Remove from the oven and allow to cool a little. Squeeze the garlic out of its skin into a small bowl and add the lemon juice and olive oil. Stir to combine. Drizzle over the vegetables and toss gently to coat. Arrange on a serving platter.

This can be served hot, warm or cold and keeps in the fridge for a day.

Buttery Garlic Cabbage

75g butter

7 cloves garlic, finely chopped

½–¾ green or savoy cabbage, thinly sliced

——

PREP 5 MINUTES   **COOK** 15 MINUTES   **SERVES** 6

Cabbage is so good for you! If you don't like it, please don't reject this recipe just yet — try my way of cooking it before you give up completely. The trick to cabbage is not to overcook it (that's when it goes all saggy and sulphury smelling — a massive shame). I used to have this as a side dish growing up and, boy, did I love it. It's just lightly sautéed with delicious garlic butter, ready in no time and a wonderful accompaniment to any dish.

Place a large frying pan over a medium-low heat. Add the butter and when it's foamy, add the garlic and cook, stirring, for a few minutes until softened and fragrant.

Put the cabbage in the pan along with ⅓ cup water. Turn the heat up to medium-high so the water simmers rapidly, and cook for about 5 minutes, stirring every now and then, until the cabbage is bright and tender — but not mushy. It should still have some bite to it. Season with salt and black pepper to taste.

My Ratatouille

3–4 tablespoons extra virgin olive oil, plus extra to drizzle

2–3 eggplants, chopped into 5cm chunks

4 courgettes, chopped into 4–5cm chunks

2–3 red capsicums, quartered

1 fennel bulb, sliced (optional)

Tomato sauce

50g butter (or ¼ cup extra virgin olive oil)

2 onions, chopped

7 cloves garlic, roughly chopped

2 tsp dried marjoram

2 tsp fresh thyme leaves (optional)

1 tsp whole fennel seeds

1 x 400g can chopped tomatoes in juice

2 tbsp tomato paste

1 tbsp red or white wine vinegar

1 tbsp brown sugar

pinch chilli flakes

¼ cup fresh basil leaves, torn

———

PREP 20 MINUTES **COOK** 35 MINUTES **SERVES** 4–6

This humble peasant-style vege dish is just so delicious — and very pretty! What's actually hiding there underneath all those beautiful vegetables is a gorgeously tasty homemade tomato sauce that adds amazing flavour to the dish when it's served up. You can serve this hot, warm or even cold.

Preheat the oven to 180°C regular bake and have a casserole or baking dish ready.

Put 1 tablespoon of the extra virgin olive oil in a frying pan over a medium-high heat. Fry the eggplant pieces until golden on one side — 1–2 minutes only. Transfer to a large bowl.

Add another tablespoon of the oil to the pan and briefly fry the courgette until just golden on both sides. Transfer to the bowl with the eggplant.

Add another tablespoon of the oil and fry the capsicum briefly until just coloured on both sides. Transfer to the bowl.

Add another tablespoon of the oil to the pan and cook the sliced fennel (if using), stirring, for a couple of minutes until softened. Transfer to the bowl.

Put the butter (or oil) in the same frying pan and reduce the heat to medium. Add the onion and cook for 10 minutes or until softened. Add the garlic, marjoram, thyme (if using) and fennel seeds and cook for another couple of minutes. Stir in the tomatoes, tomato paste, vinegar, sugar and chilli flakes. Season to taste with salt and pepper. Simmer for a couple of minutes, stir through the basil, then pour into the base of the baking dish.

Arrange the fried vegetables on top of the sauce and muddle them in nicely. Drizzle everything with a little more olive oil and season again with salt and pepper.

Bake in the preheated oven for 30–35 minutes. The vegetables should be tender but still with a little bite to them. No one likes mushy veges!

This goes really well with the slow-cooked Melting Lamb on page 122 and some nice crusty bread.

Mediterranean Salad

500g cherry tomatoes

2 whole bulbs garlic, unseparated
and unpeeled

2 tsp dried oregano

1 tsp sugar

½ cup pine nuts

1½ cups bulghur wheat

1 red onion, finely sliced

1 cup chopped mixed fresh herbs
(parsley, basil, mint, dill)

big handful Kalamata olives
(optional)

150g feta or goat's cheese,
crumbled

Dressing

3 tbsp extra virgin olive oil

1 tbsp lemon juice

1 tsp dried dill

½ tsp salt

½ tsp finely ground black pepper

___

Chelsea's tips

♥ You can make this salad with
cooked quinoa, brown rice,
buckwheat, couscous or Israeli
couscous in place of bulghur
wheat.

♥ You don't have to roast the
tomatoes if you haven't the time
or the inclination — just halve
them raw.

PREP 15 MINUTES **COOK** 30 MINUTES **SERVES** 6–8

If you haven't used bulghur wheat before, don't be afraid — it's nutritious
(low GI), super-quick to prepare, has a delicious nutty flavour and I really
love it. Basically, it's whole grains of wheat that have been cracked and
pre-cooked. You can use it anywhere you'd normally use rice, quinoa or
couscous, and you should be able to find it in any supermarket.

Preheat the oven to 180°C fan-bake.

Place the tomatoes in a medium roasting dish with the garlic bulbs. Drizzle
with olive oil, add the oregano and sugar and season with salt and pepper.
Toss to combine and roast in the oven for 30 minutes or until the garlic is
soft. Remove and allow to cool.

Lightly toast the pine nuts in a dry pan over a medium heat until golden.
Don't leave them unattended or they will burn, if you're anything like me!
Toss the pan to keep them moving. Set aside on a plate to cool.

Place the bulghur wheat in a large heatproof bowl with 1 teaspoon salt.
Add about 3 cups just-boiled water, stir and leave for about 10 minutes to
soak. When it's ready, it should be soft but with a nice firm bite to it, not
soggy. Set aside to drain in a sieve.

To make the dressing, squeeze the roasted garlic out of its skin into a small
bowl. Add the olive oil, lemon juice, dill, salt and pepper, and stir with a
fork to combine.

Put the drained bulghur wheat in a large salad bowl with the tomatoes and
their juices, onion, herbs, pine nuts and olives (if using). Pour the dressing
over the top and toss gently to combine. Just before serving, sprinkle with
the feta.

Waldorf Salad

2 baby cos lettuce (or 1 iceberg
lettuce), leaves torn

1½ cups red or green grapes

1 cup roughly chopped walnuts

2 apples, peeled and sliced into
batons

4 stalks celery, finely chopped

½ cup raisins (optional)

2 tbsp finely chopped mixed
fresh herbs (parsley, dill, basil,
fennel, chives)

Dressing

¼ cup mayonnaise

1 tbsp apple cider vinegar

1 tbsp honey

2 tsp Dijon mustard

½ tsp salt

¼ tsp finely ground white pepper

———

Chelsea's tips

♥ If you cut the apple in advance,
toss it in a little fresh lemon juice
to keep it from going brown.

PREP 15 MINUTES **SERVES** 6–8

This is my version of the much-loved, tried and true classic. A nice creamy twist on a green salad with the lovely fresh texture of apple and the buttery crunch of walnut. A few fresh herbs and you're set! And it goes with just about everything.

Place the dressing ingredients in a bowl and whisk to combine. Cover and refrigerate until needed.

In a large salad bowl, combine the lettuce with the other salad ingredients. Cover and keep in the fridge for a few hours until needed.

When you're ready to serve, gently toss through the dressing to combine.

Leftovers keep for a day in the fridge.

Asian Slaw

Dressing

⅓ cup good-quality storebought
  or homemade mayonnaise

2 tsp lime or lemon juice

1 tsp finely grated fresh ginger

1 clove garlic, crushed

1 tsp salt

¼ tsp sesame oil

¼ tsp finely ground white pepper

¼ tsp finely ground black pepper

Slaw

5 cups finely sliced cabbage
  (purple, savoy, green)

2 carrots, peeled and grated

2 sticks celery, finely sliced

½ cup chopped fresh herbs
  (coriander, mint, parsley, basil)

½ cup roasted peanuts, chopped

handful sugar snap peas, sliced

1 red chilli, finely sliced or
  chopped (optional)

zest of 1 lime or lemon

———

PREP 20 MINUTES **SERVES** 6

This fresh, colourful and super-tasty side is a favourite year-round, and will go down a real treat at any pot-luck, picnic or BBQ, or alongside any Asian-inspired meal or even as a slaw in a burger.

Place all the dressing ingredients in a bowl and stir to combine. Cover and set aside until needed.

Place the slaw ingredients in a large bowl and toss with the dressing to combine.

Leftovers keep in the fridge overnight.

BBQ Pizza Bread with Sweet Chilli & Pesto

1½ cups lukewarm water

1 tsp sugar

2 tsp active dried yeast (check the expiry date)

4 cups high-grade flour (or 'strong' bread flour)

1 tsp salt

1 tbsp extra virgin olive oil

Toppings

pesto (see page 160 or storebought)

Thai sweet chilli sauce

___

Chelsea's tips

♥ Look at the label on your yeast — if it has the word 'instant' on it, you can just add it straight to the flour. If it doesn't, it needs to be activated first.

♥ While the BBQ is definitely the most delicious way to cook this bread, you could also use the oven. Either place under a hot grill for a few minutes each side, or on a preheated pizza stone at 240°C fan-bake for 5–10 minutes. You can then char it over a gas hob for a few seconds at the very end for a smoky flavour.

PREP 20 MINUTES PLUS 1–2 HOURS RISING TIME   **COOK** 10 MINUTES   **MAKES** 4–5 PIECES

I can't even tell you how tasty this whole business is. The bread is delicious in itself — crispy, chewy and soft all at once with a lovely charred BBQ flavour, but then the flavours on top are, like, ridiculous! The bread is really easy to make, too. For a simpler topping, olive oil, salt, garlic and rosemary (or thyme) is a winner.

Combine the water, sugar and yeast in a bowl or jug, and whisk together for 10 seconds. Leave to sit for 5–10 minutes — wait until the yeast has started to go frothy on top.

Put the flour, salt and oil in a large metal or plastic mixing bowl. Add the yeast mixture and stir to form a craggy dough.

Tip out onto a clean benchtop and knead vigorously for 10 minutes until the dough is very smooth and stretchy. Put your back into it!

Place the dough back in the bowl, cover with a damp tea towel and leave somewhere warmish and draught-free until it has roughly doubled in size — it might take 1–2 hours. (You can pop it in a turned-off oven with a bowl of just-boiled water if it's very cold where you are.)

When the dough has doubled in size, remove from the bowl and divide into 4 or 5 pieces. Flatten each one to about 1cm thick, shape it how you want it, and leave on a generously floured tray out of the draught, until it starts to rise and puff up again — maybe 20 minutes or so.

Preheat a clean BBQ grill to a medium-high heat (no oil needed) and grill the bread for a few minutes each side until slightly charred and crispy. You can move it around a bit to get criss-cross lines if you like.

When cooked, smother in whatever topping you like and eat immediately — don't forget the salt and pepper!

tasty tidbits

Ah yes, the delectable misfits that don't really fit into any of the other sections, but needed to be a part of *Eat*. I reckon it's these types of recipes that are the most satisfying to make from scratch. Inside, you'll find a delightfully random assortment of deliciousness to make when it suits and when the seasons and ingredients call for it. Let me take you on a scrumptious little detour away from dinners, to share with you sauces, spreads, condiments and other gems to savour. You really have to try the freshly baked bread — and if there's a time when you have too many lemons, the Lemon Honey on homemade toast is an experience of pure happiness. Might I also add that the fresh pesto, made with fragrant late-summer basil, will restore your faith in this beautiful Italian classic. Oh, and the ketchup is sunshine in a bottle. Go for it, my friends.

Fresh Homemade Bread

300g high-grade white flour (or 'strong' bread or baker's flour)

300g wholemeal flour (stoneground organic is a lovely choice)

1 tsp salt

1¾ cups lukewarm water

2½ tsp active dried yeast (check the expiry date)

½ tsp sugar

———

Chelsea's tips

♥ Look at the label on your yeast — if it has the word 'instant' on it, you can just add it straight to the flour. If it doesn't, it needs to be activated first.

♥ If you can find 'organic bread flour', I highly recommend it in place of the high-grade white flour.

♥ It takes time to get to know the breadmaking process. If your first loaves don't turn out perfectly, don't worry about it. All bread is awesome when it's toasted — lots of avocado and some seasoning and you're all good!

PREP 20 MINUTES PLUS 3+ HOURS PROVING TIME
COOK 35–40 MINUTES **MAKES** 1 X 20CM LOAF

Making your own bread is a beautiful and rewarding process — there's magic in this ancient tradition. It's sad that bread sometimes gets a bad rap, because not all bread is created equal! Homemade tastes better, and usually it's better for you as it's free of the additives found in most commercially processed bread. This recipe isn't difficult, it just takes a little time. It's the best feeling in the world, pulling a hot fresh loaf out of your oven and devouring it warm with butter. Oh, and this bread makes the *best* toast!

Clear a space on your kitchen benchtop to do the kneading.

Place the flours and salt in a large metal or plastic mixing bowl.

Measure out the water — it should be lukewarm. Not warm like a bath, just not chilled.

To activate the yeast, pour about one-quarter of the lukewarm water into a small bowl. Add the sugar and yeast and stir briskly with a fork for 20 seconds. If some bits clump up, just let it sit for 30 seconds to soften, then stir again. Leave for 5–10 minutes until you see it start to foam on top — this means it's activated. Add the yeast mixture to the flour along with the rest of the water, and stir to bring it to a rough dough.

Tip out onto the clean benchtop — it's kneading time! This will take at least 10 minutes. You start off with a mess and end up with a smooth, supple ball of dough. Knead by pushing the dough away from you with firm pressure from the heel of your hand, then grabbing it and bringing it back by folding it back over itself. What you're essentially doing is stretching out the gluten strands so the dough can rise properly and not turn out like a brick. It will start off sticky and messy, but just keep going. Rub your hands together to get any excess dough off, and don't be tempted to add more flour. As you knead, the dough should become less sticky. You will be tired — I sort of perch on one foot and put my bodyweight into each knead. It's a good workout, and at the same time you're putting all your own clean energy into the loaf.

To test if it's ready, try to gently stretch out a chunk of the dough as thin as possible with your fingers — when the dough is ready, it should stretch enough that you can see light through it. If it's not ready, it will just tear. You'll get there eventually — just keep kneading until you do.

When ready, put the dough back into the mixing bowl (unwashed is fine) and pop a plastic shopping bag loosely over the top. Leave it in a place free of draughts until the dough has doubled in size. Keep in mind that there's not an exact time for this to happen. It will happen fastest in ideal conditions of humidity and 22–27°C — but it will always rise eventually, if

Recipe continued over page . . .

cooler. In summer, you'll be fine. In winter, a hot-water cupboard or warm room is good, or you can place the dough in a turned-off oven with a tray of just-boiled water. Make sure the temperature doesn't go above 60°C or the yeast will die. If it's very warm, and the dough doubles in size very quickly — say 30 minutes — punch it back down again and let it start over.

Lightly grease a 20cm loaf tin with butter or oil.

Scrape the risen dough out on the bench (you shouldn't need any more flour) and roll it into a log that's double the length of your loaf tin. Use your knuckles to squash the log flat, then fold it up in three. Use your knuckles to squash it down again into a flattened chunky rectangle. Now, roll the rectangle up from the short end (it's okay if the ends stick out).

Place in the loaf tin with the seam-side down. Cover again with the plastic bag (in a way that the loaf won't touch it as it rises) and leave in the same place again until the loaf has risen to almost twice the size again (approximately 1–2 hours), and looks puffy and like a proper loaf of bread. Sprinkle with flour if you like.

Preheat the oven to 220°C regular bake.

Put the risen dough in the preheated oven and immediately turn the temperature down to 200°C. Bake for 35–40 minutes — it should sound hollow when lightly tapped.

Remove from the oven. Leave to cool for a few minutes, then remove from the tin and cool on a wire rack to prevent it going soggy.

Your beautiful bread is best eaten warm with butter or as a sandwich the same day — after that I prefer it toasted.

Hey Pesto!

3 cups packed fresh basil leaves

¼ cup pine nuts (untoasted)

2 cloves fresh New Zealand garlic, peeled

1½ tsp salt

1 tbsp fresh lemon juice

½ cup freshly grated Parmesan (see below for note)

½ cup grated Pecorino cheese

80ml cold pressed, extra virgin olive oil (soft and smooth flavour is good)

——

Chelsea's tips

♥ You can use peanuts instead of pine nuts for a slightly different flavour — a good option if there are no pine nuts in the house!

Important stuff

♥ Feel free to use a large mortar and pestle instead of a food processor (use circular motions for the basil part).

♥ Use good-quality ingredients for this recipe. Extra virgin olive oil, and fresh New Zealand garlic. Please, I beg of you, don't use Parmesan that comes pre-grated in a bag — or worse, the powdered kind that smells like old socks. A hard block you grate yourself with a fine plane/grater is the best.

♥ If you can find an aged Parmesan called 'Parmigiano-Reggiano', it's a little more expensive but it's legit from Italy. (Not essential at all, but good to know.)

♥ Pecorino is a delicious sheep's milk cheese similar to Parmesan; it adds a lovely subtle tang. You can get it in most supermarkets now, but if not, using extra Parmesan is fine.

PREP 15 MINUTES **MAKES** ABOUT 300ML

On one of my tours of Italy, I was lucky enough to visit the seaside town of Porto Venere. It was like a postcard — cute coloured houses precariously stacked on a hill, quaint cobbled streets, tasty seafood restaurants — and tucked away in a little alley was a shop that made and sold the best pesto I'd ever tasted. Very soft and creamy, a bright vibrant green with a fresh tang — you can't buy pesto like that in New Zealand. This recipe is as close as I can get to it — it's like a sunny Mediterranean summer in a jar.

Have an airtight container or a clean jar with a lid ready to transfer the pesto into.

Gently rinse the basil leaves under cold water and lay on a clean tea towel to dry — try not to bruise or crush them. If you have any big leaves, you may need to tear them gently into smaller pieces for the food processor (don't use a knife). Remove any stems as they can be bitter.

Place the pine nuts, garlic and salt in a small to medium-sized food processor. Pulse until you have a rough paste. Add the basil leaves and lemon juice and pulse until the basil is all incorporated into a bright green paste (you'll probably need to prod and scrape the sides with a spatula every now and then). I still like a little texture, so not too fine, but no huge chunks of basil either. Add the cheeses and pulse a few times until just combined.

Scrape the mixture into a bowl and add the oil in a thin stream, stirring all the time until incorporated. Season with pepper — and extra salt if you like.

Spoon into the airtight container or jar. The less exposure the mixture has to the air, the better. Pour a layer of olive oil on top to help keep air out. Keeps in the fridge for a couple of weeks. It can also be frozen for 3–4 months.

Excellent tossed through fresh pasta with tomatoes, tossed through roasted vegetables, dolloped on soup, on crostini or bruschetta, or spread on crackers or fresh baked bread as part of a platter. It's very nice on a slice of my Fresh Homemade Bread on page 156!

Romesco Sauce

3 large red capsicums

1 whole bulb garlic, unseparated and unpeeled

500–600g very red ripe tomatoes

⅔ cup extra virgin olive oil

2 red onions, roughly chopped

½ tsp chilli flakes (or 1 large red chilli, chopped)

2 thick slices toast bread, torn (artisan bread like ciabatta is best)

3 tsp brown sugar

2 tsp salt

1 tsp finely ground black pepper

½ cup whole hazelnuts, roughly chopped

½ cup whole almonds, roughly chopped

1 cup chopped fresh coriander, leaves and stalks

2 tsp red wine vinegar or lemon juice

——

PREP 20 MINUTES **COOK** 40 MINUTES **SERVES** 8–10 AS A CONDIMENT

Romesco is of Spanish origin, and I reckon it could be one of the tastiest little numbers around. Once you've made a batch, you can use it as a beautiful condiment for steak, chicken, fish and pork. Just cook the meat as usual, dollop a spoonful of Romesco on the side and you're done (it doesn't need to be cooked again). Or you can toss it through cooked veges, potatoes or pasta for an instant flavour super-boost!

Preheat the oven (or a BBQ grill) to grill on high. Grill the capsicums whole, turning until they are charred and blackened all over — and I mean totally blackened. Transfer to a plastic bag, twist to seal it up and set aside for 10 minutes.

Drizzle the garlic bulb in a little olive oil and wrap in foil.

Change the oven temperature to 180°C fan-bake. Chop the tomatoes into quarters, discarding any white cores and seeds. Place in a large mixing bowl with the olive oil, onion, chilli, bread, sugar, salt and pepper, and toss to combine. Tip it all out onto an oven tray with the wrapped garlic and roast in the oven for 15 minutes.

Add the nuts to the tray and cook for another 15 minutes. Remove from the oven and leave to cool.

Remove the capsicums from the bag, pull the skins off and discard along with the seeds and stalks. Don't be tempted to rinse them! Place the roasted flesh in a food processor.

Squeeze the roasted garlic out of its skin into the food processor and add the other roasted goodies. Add the coriander and vinegar or lemon juice. Process until you have a coarse texture — not too chunky though. Season to taste with salt if it needs it, or extra lemon juice.

Keeps in an airtight container or jar in the fridge for a week — cover with a thin layer of olive oil to keep it fresh.

Ketchup

PREP 15 MINUTES   **COOK** 1 HOUR   **MAKES** 1 LITRE

2kg very ripe red tomatoes
3 tbsp olive oil
2 onions, chopped
3 cloves garlic
½ tsp allspice
½ tsp mustard powder
½ tsp ground ginger
¼ tsp ground cloves
⅓ cup tomato paste
2 tbsp malt vinegar
¼ cup brown sugar
2 tsp salt
½ tsp finely ground black pepper
½ tsp finely ground white pepper

———

Chelsea's tips

♥ You will need a 1-litre preserving jar or multiple smaller ones. You can get Perfit jars with a screw band and dome seal at the supermarket.

I'm stoked with this recipe! It's a terrific way to use up the glut of luscious late summer tomatoes — and it's seriously easy to make and way better than bought stuff. Feel free to double or even triple the recipe if you want to make enough ketchup to see your family through the winter. It jazzes up even the simplest of meals — last night we had sausages with the smashed potatoes on page 134, steamed broccoli and a good splodge of this ketchup — perfection!

Cut an X in the base of each tomato and place in a heatproof bowl. Boil the jug and pour boiling water over the tomatoes to cover them. Leave for 5 minutes, then drain the water. When cool enough to handle, pull the skins off the tomatoes and discard. Chop roughly and discard the hard white parts.

Heat the oil in a large saucepan over a medium heat. Add the onion and cook, stirring, for about 10 minutes until soft. Add the garlic and cook for 1 minute. Add the spices and cook for another minute.

Add the chopped tomatoes, tomato paste, vinegar, sugar, salt and peppers to the pan. Cover and bring to a gentle simmer for about 25 minutes. Remove the lid and let simmer for 15–20 minutes — enough to thicken to a nice sauce consistency.

Preserving the ketchup

To sterilise the jars, preheat the oven to 120°C regular bake. Line a baking tray with baking paper. Sit the jars on top and place the tray in the oven for 15 minutes. (If you have a metal ladle or serving spoon with no plastic in it, you can put it in the oven too.)

Have a chopping board ready on the bench and cover with a folded sheet of newspaper or an old (but clean) tea towel. Have another board for the saucepan to sit on.

Meanwhile, put the screw bands and dome seals in a medium saucepan. Cover with water and bring to the boil to sterilise them. Add your ladle or spoon when it's boiling, if you haven't used the oven.

Sit the saucepan of hot ketchup on the chopping board.

Remove the jars from the oven with oven mitts or a tea towel and set on the covered board. Carefully ladle the sauce into the jars, up to the top.

Wipe the jar rim with a paper towel dipped in the hot water from the saucepan so it's clear of sauce and seeds.

Carefully place the seal on, then screw the band over the top. Set upside down overnight.

To check if it's sealed, press the top — it should have sucked down. Once sealed it will keep for a few months in a cool, dark place.

Sticky Slow-roasted Cherry Tomatoes

500g very ripe cherry tomatoes
2 tbsp extra virgin olive oil
2 tsp brown sugar
1 tsp salt
pinch chilli flakes

———

Chelsea's tips

♥ You can also use very ripe large tomatoes that have been deseeded and quartered.

PREP 5 MINUTES   **COOK** 1 HOUR 20 MINUTES   **MAKES** A SMALL JAR

I am addicted to these! They're a lot more subtle and tender than sundried tomatoes, but they still pack a flavour punch! These are best at the end of summer when there is an abundance of beautiful, cheap, ripe tomatoes. They are good with just about everything — on platters, sandwiches, as a condiment with a meal, tossed through hot cooked pasta with a little pesto, on crackers . . .

Preheat the oven to 130°C regular bake. Line a small roasting dish with baking paper.

Halve the tomatoes and arrange in the roasting dish.

Combine the oil, sugar, salt and chilli in a small bowl. Pour over the tomatoes and toss to coat as best as possible.

Bake in the preheated oven for about 1 hour 20 minutes, or until very sticky and starting to caramelise. Leave to cool fully before storing for up to a week in an airtight container with the cooking oil.

Homemade Breadcrumbs

slices of not-too-fresh bread
(about 1cm)

——

PREP 5 MINUTES **COOK** 30–60 MINUTES

This might seem like a silly recipe to put in a book, but I actually think it's a neat thing to do — it's a great way to use up the end crusts of bread that nobody wants, you get a better flavour and it's so easy. I find that bought breadcrumbs can go stale very quickly and acquire a nasty taste. You can use fresh bread or slightly stale — whatever you have.

Preheat the oven to 130°C regular bake.

Arrange slices of bread on a baking or roasting tray in a single layer and bake in the preheated oven for about 30–60 minutes, or until very dry and crunchy.

If you're using a heavy grain-based bread like Vogel's or homemade, it could take longer — just keep testing. You want them dried, not golden. The drier the bread is, the longer the crumbs will keep and the crunchier they will be. If you can feel some stretchiness or softness, pop the bread back in. Keep in mind the bread will get crispier as it cools, too.

Cool the bread, then break into small pieces and place in a food processor. Process to a fine crumb.

Store in a sealed airtight container in a cool dark place for a few weeks, or freeze for up to 3 months.

Lemon Honey

1 free-range egg
3 free-range egg yolks
zest of 5 medium lemons
¾ cup lemon juice
1 cup sugar
½ tsp salt
75g butter, cubed

———

Chelsea's tips

To sterilise jars

♥ Place the jars on a lined baking tray and bake in a 120°C oven for about 10 minutes.

Boil the lids (or the screw bands and seals) in a saucepan of water just when you are ready to use them.

Place a folded piece of newspaper on a chopping board.

Carefully remove the jars from the oven, place on the newspaper-covered board and fill with the lemon honey. Carefully screw a boiled lid on top, and leave to cool completely — the lid should suck itself down, which means it's sealed.

PREP 5 MINUTES **COOK** 15 MINUTES **MAKES** ONE 500ML JAR

Sort of like a lemon curd, but more of a spread — this recipe reminds me of my childhood. We'd eat it on hot buttered toast as a treat during summer (and off the spoon out of the jar when no one was looking, to be honest — sorry Mum). It's also delicious dolloped on scones, loaves, fresh bread and desserts. This version is very tangy, I like a good lemon hit!

Place the egg and yolks in a medium-sized heatproof mixing bowl (either glass or ceramic, or metal if that's all you have).

Add the lemon zest and juice, sugar and salt and immediately whisk to combine.

Choose a saucepan that fits the bowl nicely on top of it, so most of the base is in the pan but not anywhere near the bottom. Fill the pan with about 5cm of water and place over a medium heat.

Place the bowl on top of the saucepan and when the water starts to simmer underneath, start stirring constantly with a whisk, until the mixture thickens. This might take 5–10 minutes. Don't whisk the mixture as you would egg whites — just stir briskly.

When the mixture has thickened nicely, whisk the butter in, one cube at a time. Remove from the heat.

Transfer the mixture to an airtight container, or if you want it to look nice or to give it as a gift, put it in a sterilised jar (see Chelsea's tips). You can get nice little preserving jars from the supermarket these days.

Keeps in an airtight container in the fridge for a month or so.

treatsome

It's official — homemade treats bring real happiness into the world. And I kinda feel like life would be a pretty sad time without a few baked goodies in the mix to spruce things up. Inside this section you'll find a delectable sweet to suit whatever you're in the mood for. I've got biscuits, desserts, puddings, buns, cakes and, for some reason, four loaf recipes. Yep, loaves are the new thing — you heard it here first. I've also really gone to town with no-bake slices (there are four of those, too) for times when preheating the oven just feels like far too much effort. For the ultimate in decadent desserts, wait till you try the Chocolate Hazelnut Cheesecake. Mamma mia, it's a ripper and a great one if you're entertaining. I think my personal favourites would have to be the Chocolate Orange Sherbert Slice and the Gingernuts. But I invite you to try as many of these recipes as you can and let me know which ones you love the most.

Macaroons

2 cups shredded coconut

1½ cups desiccated coconut

1 x 395g can sweetened condensed milk

1 tsp pure vanilla extract

½ tsp salt

3 free-range egg whites

150g chocolate, chopped

___

Chelsea's tips

♥ You can make my Lemon Honey with the leftover yolks — the recipe is on page 170.

PREP 5–10 MINUTES **COOK** 17–20 MINUTES **MAKES** ABOUT 15

I am so in love with how amazingly easy this recipe is — the mixture is done and in the oven in about 5 minutes flat. The result is a whole lot of gorgeously golden, coconutty puffs with chocolate bottoms. Just utter deliciousness. Also, anything that contains a whole can of sweetened condensed milk simply has to be a winner.

Preheat the oven to 160°C regular bake. Line a baking tray with baking paper (you might need two trays, or you can make them in two batches).

Place the shredded and desiccated coconut, condensed milk, vanilla and salt in a large mixing bowl. Stir with a fork until evenly combined into a sticky mixture.

In a clean medium-sized mixing bowl, beat the egg whites until firm peaks form (when you turn the beater upside down, the little peak of egg white should stand up fairly firmly). This won't take long — under a minute even with a hand-powered egg beater.

Gently fold the egg white mixture into the coconut mixture with a spatula until evenly combined.

Dollop spoonfuls 4cm apart on the baking tray/s. Bake in the preheated oven for 17–20 minutes, or until just turning light golden all over. You don't want them overcooked or they will go dry.

Remove from the oven and allow to cool completely. Cook the other batch if you need to.

Place the chocolate in a microwave-proof (glass or ceramic) bowl and microwave on high for 1 minute. Stir until melted. Dunk the bottom of each macaroon in the chocolate and set upside-down on the tray until the chocolate has set.

These will keep in an airtight container at room temperature for a few days or until they're gobbled up.

Gluten- & Dairy-free Banana Chocolate Chip Pancakes

PREP 10 MINUTES **COOK** 20 MINUTES **SERVES** 6

2 cups gluten-free flour mix (without raising agent added)

2 tsp baking powder (check to ensure that it's gluten-free if necessary)

1 tsp baking soda

½ tsp fine sea salt

5 free-range eggs

2 tbsp sugar

1½ cups coconut milk (cow's milk works fine, too, if you don't need it to be dairy-free)

2 tbsp lemon juice (or apple cider/white vinegar)

2 tsp pure vanilla extract

2 ripe bananas, mashed

1 cup chopped dark (dairy-free) chocolate

———

These are gluten- and dairy-free, but you don't need to be to enjoy them! My standard hotcakes from *Everyday Delicious* have been such a hit, I decided to create another version for all my gluten- and dairy-intolerant pals out there (because it's not just a matter of substituting like for like). Many good-quality chocolate brands with over 50% cocoa solids are dairy-free in New Zealand — take a look on the label or ask them (leave the chocolate out if in doubt). Crispy bacon and sliced banana with maple syrup is a great topping for these.

Sift the flour, baking powder, baking soda and salt into a large mixing bowl. Stir with a whisk to combine. Make a well in the centre and set aside.

Put the eggs and sugar in a medium-sized mixing bowl and beat until fluffy — about 15 seconds with an electric beater on medium; 30 seconds with a hand-operated egg beater; or 1 minute with a whisk.

Pour the egg mixture, coconut milk, lemon juice (or vinegar), vanilla and banana into the well in the dry ingredients. Stir gently with a whisk from the centre in a circular motion until smooth and combined. Stir through the chocolate.

Heat a large (preferably non-stick) frying pan over a medium/medium-low heat. The pan is ready when you flick a few drops of water in it and they dance around a bit.

To get the smooth, even look on your pancakes, don't use butter in the pan. If your pan is really sticky, though, you might have to. Sometimes I use butter to cook the first one to get the pan seasoned for the rest of them (the first one is often a dud anyway).

I use about ½ cup of the mixture for each pancake — you can use less if you want them smaller like pikelets, or more if you want them massive. Allow space in the pan for them to spread a little. You can thin the mixture down a little if you feel it's too thick, using 2 tablespoons of water or coconut milk.

Cook the pancakes for 30–60 seconds, or until bubbles start to pop up on the surface and leave little holes, then turn over. They will puff up now. Cook for another 1–2 minutes until cooked through, then stack on a plate. (Keep warm in a 50°C oven while you cook the rest, if you like.) Repeat until the mixture is used up. You will get a feel for how hot the pan needs to be and how long you cook them for after you have cooked a couple.

Serve with your favourite things — lemon juice and icing sugar, berries, coconut yoghurt, chopped pecans or walnuts, maple syrup (a must for me), sliced banana — even bacon.

Gingernuts

150g butter, cubed
1⅓ cups brown sugar
¼ cup golden syrup
2¼ cups plain flour
4 tbsp ground ginger
½ tsp baking soda
¾ tsp salt
1 free-range egg
2 tsp pure vanilla extract

——

Chelsea's tips

♥ The firmness of the biscuits will depend on how long they are cooked. The less time and lighter the colour, the softer they will be — play around until you get it right for your oven so they are how you like them.

PREP 15 MINUTES PLUS 30–60 MINUTES CHILLING TIME
COOK ABOUT 15 MINUTES **MAKES** 12–16 BISCUITS

Hot damn, there's just nothing quite like a spicy gingernut dunked in a nice hot cup of tea. I played around with this recipe for days until I finally got it right. Don't fret if yours don't come out exactly like mine — there's always a lot of variance with baking. You can play with the sizes of the biscuits and the cooking times until you get it perfect — it's all part of the fun.

Preheat the oven to 170°C regular bake. Set a rack in the centre of the oven. Line a large baking tray with baking paper.

Place the butter, sugar and golden syrup in a saucepan over a medium heat. Stir constantly until melted and combined evenly (the sugar doesn't have to be dissolved). Transfer to a bowl to cool.

Sift the flour, ginger, baking soda and salt into a large mixing bowl and stir to combine.

Whisk the egg and vanilla through the cooled butter mixture. Add to the flour mixture and stir with a wooden spoon to combine.

Cover and refrigerate for 30–60 minutes.

Roll into balls (start with slightly heaped tablespoons, about 35–40g) and arrange on the baking tray 6cm apart — they will spread.

Bake in the preheated oven for 15–20 minutes, or until dark golden brown. Cool on a wire rack.

Keep in an airtight container at room temperature for a week. I prefer them after a day or so when they have softened a little bit. But hard is good for dunking!

Sweet Pea Cake

2½ cups plain flour

1½ tsp baking powder

½ tsp salt

225g butter, at room temperature

2 cups caster sugar

3 free-range eggs, at room temperature

3 tsp vanilla essence

zest of 1 orange or lemon

1¼ cups milk, warmed to skin temperature

flowers, to garnish (edible if possible)

Natural pink icing

200g butter, softened slightly

2½ cups icing sugar

¼ cup cornflour

pinch salt

1 tsp natural orange essence

½ beetroot

Chelsea's tips

♥ You can use red food colouring if you don't have any beetroot on hand.

♥ A beautiful fresh way to finish the cake is with some pretty flowers — they could be from your garden (or your neighbour's!). I used sweet peas on mine when I first made it, hence the name. However, sweet pea flowers are not edible.

PREP 15 MINUTES **COOK** 1 HOUR 15 MINUTES **SERVES** 8–10

You guys are always asking for a good recipe for a vanilla cake with buttercream — for birthdays, bridal parties, baby showers and all those exciting celebratory times in life that call for a gorgeous cake. I obeyed! It's prettily pink, and the best part is I've used beetroot juice in the icing rather than nasty old red food colouring (no, you can't taste the beetroot). The cake itself is lovely and buttery and stays soft for a few days. The whole thing has a very subtle citrus flavour which I think gives it something a bit special, too.

Preheat the oven to 160°C regular bake. Line the base and sides of a 24cm cake tin with baking paper.

Sift the flour, baking powder and salt into a medium-sized bowl, stir to combine with a whisk, and set aside.

Cream the butter and sugar with an electric beater (or cake mixer) on medium-high speed for 5–7 minutes — it needs to turn very pale and fluffy. Scrape the sides clean with a spatula.

Add the eggs, one at a time, beating on medium speed for 30 seconds after each addition. Scrape down the sides again. Add the vanilla essence and orange or lemon zest and beat for another 15 seconds.

Sift in one-third of the flour mixture, then mix on the lowest speed just long enough for the flour to be incorporated. Add one-third of the milk, and do the same. Repeat these two steps until all the flour mixture and milk is used up — scrape down the sides again as you go. At the end, the mixture should be smooth (if it looks a little curdled, that's fine). Take care not to over-mix the batter at this point, as it can let air out of the mixture and toughen the cake. Scrape the batter into the prepared tin and smooth out.

Bake in the preheated oven for 1 hour 15 minutes — a skewer inserted into the centre should come out clean. Cool in the tin for 10 minutes, then remove and cool completely on a wire rack before icing.

Natural pink icing

Place the butter, icing sugar, cornflour and salt in a large mixing bowl (or the bowl of your cake mixer). Beat for a few minutes until the mixture is very light and fluffy and whipped-looking. Beat in the orange essence.

Grate the beetroot and squeeze the juice out into a small bowl. Add 1 teaspoon of juice at a time to the icing until you are happy with the colour. I iced my cake using a warm butter knife — I'm not very fancy.

Keeps for a couple of days in an airtight container.

Chocolate Orange Sherbet Slice

Base

250g malt biscuits
100g butter, very soft
¾ cup rolled oats
⅓ cup sweetened condensed milk
zest of 1 orange
¼ tsp salt

Topping

500g dark chocolate, chopped (about 50–60% cocoa)
250ml cream
zest of 3–4 oranges
100g butter, cubed
1 tsp natural orange essence
½ tsp salt

Sherbet

zest of 2 oranges, plus extra to sprinkle
½ cup icing sugar
½ tsp tartaric acid
¼ tsp citric acid
¼ tsp salt

———

Chelsea's tips

♥ You can flag the sherbet part if you like and simply sprinkle with a mixture of the icing sugar and orange zest — it will still be delicious.

PREP 20 MINUTES PLUS 4+ HOURS SETTING TIME **MAKES** 20 PIECES

My favourite sweet in the book! I'm a choc-orange fiend and I've been wanting to create a jaffa-type slice for ages now. I wasn't quite sure where I was heading when I started out, but eventually things clicked into place and here we are. The silky richness of the chocolate fudgy part is balanced by the tart sherbet — a zing in every bite! You'll have quite a few oranges left sitting naked and vulnerable after you've made this. I just squeeze mine and we drink the juice with a few cubes of ice at breakfast.

Line a 20cm square slice tin with baking paper so it goes up the sides.

Crumble the biscuits into a food processor. Process to a fine crumb. Add the remaining base ingredients and process to combine (I find tilting the processor helps it blend better). If you don't have a food processor, you can smash the biscuits up in a clean tea towel with a rolling pin and then mix the other ingredients in afterwards.

Press the crumb firmly in an even layer into the prepared tin. Set aside.

Put the chocolate, cream and orange zest in a glass or ceramic mixing bowl and microwave on high for 1 minute 30 seconds. Stir to melt the chocolate. You can pop it in for another minute or so if it needs it. Add the butter and stir briskly to combine.

Lastly, stir through the orange essence and salt. Spread the topping over the base.

To make the sherbet, either blitz everything in a small food processor or finely chop the zest and combine with the other ingredients in a bowl.

Sprinkle over the chocolate topping, add the extra zest, cover and refrigerate for at least 4 hours until firm, then slice. You'll have extra sherbet, so either sprinkle on some more when serving the slice, or keep in a container and just stick your finger in and eat it every now and then.

Keep this slice in the fridge as the topping will go soft in warm weather. It will keep in an airtight container for up to a week. You can also freeze it.

Pumpkin Pie Loaf

700g pumpkin (about 500g once peeled and deseeded)

125g butter, at room temperature

1½ cups brown sugar

2 free-range eggs, at room temperature

2 tsp pure vanilla extract

2 cups plain flour

1 tbsp ground ginger

½ tsp ground cinnamon

½ tsp ground nutmeg

2 tsp baking powder

½ tsp baking soda

½ tsp salt

¼ tsp finely ground white or black pepper

Chelsea's tips

♥ To speed up cooling the pumpkin, spread it across a dinner plate and pop in the freezer or fridge.

♥ You can also microwave the pumpkin pieces on high for 5 minutes, with ¼ cup water in a covered glass or ceramic bowl, if you like.

PREP 30 MINUTES **COOK** 1 HOUR 10 MINUTES **SERVES** 8–10

Oh, how I love this recipe! It was inspired by one in Dame Alison Holst's big red book — I must have made it a kajillion times when I was growing up and that page of the book was all gummed up with loaf mixture. (I really hope that happens to you with this recipe.) I've added a few little flourishes of my own and ramped up the ginger and spices . . . someone actually said 'it tastes like pumpkin pie in a loaf!' — that was good enough for me.

Preheat the oven to 160°C regular bake and set a rack just below the centre of the oven. Line a loaf tin (about 23cm x 10cm) with baking paper so it goes up and past the sides by about a centimetre.

Peel the pumpkin, discard the seeds and pith and cut into even chunks about 4cm wide. Place in a small/medium saucepan, fill with water to just cover the pumpkin, cover with a lid and simmer for 10–15 minutes until soft. Drain well. Either mash finely, press through a sieve with a spatula, or use a food processor to make a purée. Leave to cool. You need one generous cup of purée for the loaf.

Cream the butter and sugar for a few minutes until pale and fluffy. Add the eggs, one at a time, beating well after each addition. Beat in the vanilla.

Sift the flour into another mixing bowl with the spices, baking powder, baking soda, salt and pepper. Stir well to combine.

Sift half the flour mixture into the creamed mixture, then fold to just combine, using a rubber spatula to scrape the sides as you go. Gently fold through half the pumpkin purée to just combine. Repeat the process with the remaining flour mixture and pumpkin. Scrape the mixture into the prepared tin.

Bake in the preheated oven for 1 hour and 10 minutes, or until a skewer inserted into the loaf comes out clean. Leave to cool for 10 minutes in the tin, then turn out onto a wire rack. Cool completely before slicing; it will cut easier. Waiting may prove difficult, though. I love this loaf sliced and buttered with a piping hot Earl Grey tea. Yum!

Banana Chocolate Chip Muffins

½ cup milk

1 tbsp lemon juice

200g butter, cubed

¾ cup brown sugar

2 cups plain flour

3 tsp baking powder

¼ tsp baking soda

¼ tsp salt

2 free-range eggs

2 tsp pure vanilla extract

2 very ripe medium bananas, mashed

¾ cup chopped dark chocolate or chocolate chips

———

Chelsea's tips

♥ To make these as mini muffins, reduce the cooking time to about 10–15 minutes.

PREP 15 MINUTES **COOK** 20–25 MINUTES **MAKES** 12–16 MUFFINS

This is another recipe I get asked for a lot — it's just a good old, simple banana choc chip muffin that's not trying to be too healthy or fancy. Yeah, I reckon the bran and honey can take a hike this time. These are absolutely scrumptious, and they are really easy to make so are a good one for the kids to help out with — just melt, stir and go! I didn't use muffin cases for these, I just buttered and floured the tins, old-school style. It's up to you what you do.

Preheat the oven to 180°C fan-bake. Grease a 12-pan muffin tray and dust with flour. Shake out the excess.

Pour the milk and lemon juice into a non-metallic bowl or mug and leave to sit for a few minutes until needed — it will go thick and curdled.

Melt the butter and brown sugar in a small saucepan over a medium-low heat until only just melted (or microwave in a glass or ceramic bowl for 90 seconds on high). Remove from the heat.

Sift the flour, baking powder, baking soda and salt into a mixing bowl and stir to combine.

Break the eggs into another mixing bowl and beat until smooth. Add the melted butter and sugar, sour milk mixture and vanilla, and whisk to combine evenly.

Make a well in the flour mixture and pour in the wet mixture. Using a whisk, stir gently from the centre in a circular motion until it all comes together to form a batter — it won't go completely smooth, so don't over-mix it. Fold through the banana and chocolate.

Fill the muffin pans to the top (you may need to cook the muffins in two batches).

Bake in the preheated oven for 20–25 minutes until risen and golden. Cool for 15 minutes in the tray before trying to get them out.

These muffins can be frozen once cooled, and popped in lunchboxes in the morning to thaw in time for morning tea.

Nutty Banana & Cinnamon Loaf

200g butter, at room
temperature, cubed

¾ cup brown sugar

⅓ cup honey

2 large ripe bananas, roughly
mashed or chopped

⅓ cup milk

1 free-range egg

1 free-range egg yolk

2 tsp pure vanilla extract or paste

1 tsp apple cider or white vinegar

¾ cup whole nuts (walnuts,
pecans, almonds, Brazils)

2 cups plain flour (gluten-free
flour mix works well too)

1 tbsp ground cinnamon

2 tsp baking powder

½ tsp baking soda

½ tsp salt

___

Chelsea's tips

♥ For a dairy-free option, use
½ cup grapeseed oil in place of
butter, and ⅓ cup coconut milk
in place of milk.

PREP 10 MINUTES **COOK** 1 HOUR **SERVES** 8–10

Here's a nice twist on a regular banana loaf — it's a simple and delish way
to use up those sad, saggy and spotty bananas sitting in your fruit bowl.
The best part is, while it's baking your kitchen will be filled with the warm
aromas of cinnamon, buttery bananas and lightly toasted nuts. Yummage!

Preheat the oven to 160°C regular bake and set a rack in the centre of the
oven. Line a loaf tin (about 23cm x 10cm) with baking paper so it sticks up
over the sides a few centimetres.

Melt the butter, brown sugar and honey in a small saucepan over a
medium-low heat, or microwave for 1 minute in a glass bowl. Stir to mix.
Stir through the banana, milk, egg and yolk, vanilla and vinegar.

Finely chop the nuts (you can pulse them in a processor) and place in a
large mixing bowl. Sift in the flour, cinnamon, baking powder, baking soda
and salt. Stir to combine.

Pour in the banana mixture and stir until you have a smooth batter that's
evenly mixed. Scrape the mixture into the prepared tin.

Bake in the preheated oven for 1 hour, or until a skewer inserted into the
centre comes out clean.

Leave to cool in the tin for 10 minutes, then turn out onto a wire rack. Serve
warm or cold, with a smear of butter if you like.

Keeps in an airtight container at room temperature for a few days.

Hot Cross Buns

Fruit

zest and juice of 2 oranges

1½ cups raisins, sultanas, chopped dried apricots or a mixture

Super booster

1¼ cups high-grade white flour

1½ cups milk

2 tbsp sugar

3 tsp active dried yeast (check expiry date)

Dough

3 cups high-grade white flour

3 tbsp brown sugar

2 tbsp mixed spice

1 tsp ground cinnamon

½ tsp ground cloves

1 tsp salt

50g chilled butter

1 free-range egg, lightly beaten

Crosses

½ cup plain flour

1 tbsp sugar

½ tsp baking powder

⅓ cup cold water

Glaze

½ cup sugar

⅓ cup just-boiled water

PREP 30 MINUTES PLUS 1–2+ HOURS SOAKING TIME AND 3–4 HOURS RISING TIME **COOK** 15–20 MINUTES **MAKES** 16 BUNS

These are not at all hard to make but, like all good bread recipes, they take a little time. To get the buns super light and soft, you make a yeast 'super booster' at the start to get it all going. It adds a smidgeon more time to the process, but it's so worth it. And you probably only make hot cross buns once a year, so what's your rush?

Fruit

Heat the orange zest and juice in a small saucepan until hot. Place the dried fruit in a bowl or a resealable bag and pour the orange juice in. Cover or seal, and leave for 1–2 hours or overnight. Drain the fruit in a sieve before using.

Super booster

Put the flour in a large mixing bowl.

Pour the milk into a microwave-proof (glass or ceramic) bowl and microwave in 20-second bursts until it reaches skin temperature — about 32°C is ideal. If it gets too warm, just let it cool down to skin temperature before using. Add the sugar and yeast to the milk, and whisk gently for 20 seconds or so.

Make a well in the flour and pour in the milk mixture, stirring to combine evenly. Cover with a clean damp cloth or a plastic bag, and leave somewhere draught-free for however long it takes for it to double in size (see Dough-rising tips over the page).

Dough

Once the super booster has risen, put the flour, sugar, spices and salt in a large metal or plastic mixing bowl and stir. The bowl needs to be big enough for the dough to double in size later.

Finely chop the chilled butter and add to the flour mixture along with the super booster and egg. Stir with a wooden spoon to bring it all together into a rough dough.

Tip out onto a clean benchtop. Start to knead — it will feel very wet and sticky at first and your hands will feel caked in dough. You can rub your hands in a little more flour to clean them, adding the crumbs back to the dough. Keep kneading — eventually, the dough will stop sticking to your hands and the bench so much. Don't be tempted to add heaps of flour — a little bit at the start is okay, but a sticky dough will produce *much* better buns than a dry dough.

Recipe continued over page . . .

Hot Cross Buns continued . . .

Knead firmly for another 10 minutes — it needs to be very smooth and stretchy (see Kneading tips opposite). Once it's ready, leave to sit for 5–10 minutes to relax before adding the fruit.

Drain the fruit well in a sieve and tip onto the benchtop. Squash the dough out on top and knead it all together for another minute or so. It will feel slippery and weird to start with — just persist with gentle kneading and it will all come back together into a cohesive, very sticky dough eventually.

Place the dough back in the mixing bowl, pop a plastic bag on top and leave in a draught-free place (see Dough-rising tips opposite) until it's doubled in size — usually an hour or two — it depends on the temperature of the surroundings, among other things. It's a visual clue, not a timed one.

When it's doubled in size, tip out onto a clean benchtop and divide into 16 even pieces (you can weigh them if you have electric scales). Firmly roll each portion until you have a fairly smooth ball.

Line a baking tray or metal baking dish with baking paper (mine was about 30cm x 20cm). Place the balls 1–2cm apart on the tray. My buns were pretty much touching to start with, so they all joined up nicely as they rose.

Cover with lightly oiled cling wrap and leave to rise again for another hour or so until puffed up into proper bun size — they don't rise any more when cooking, like cakes do.

Preheat the oven to 180°C fan-bake and set a rack in the centre of the oven.

Crosses

Stir the flour, sugar, baking powder and water together with a fork to form a smooth paste. Place in a piping bag with a small round nozzle (or a ziplock bag with a tiny corner cut off). Pipe thin crosses on top of each bun.

Bake immediately in the preheated oven for about 15–20 minutes, or until golden brown all over.

Glaze

While the buns are cooking, whisk the sugar and just-boiled water in a microwave-proof (glass or ceramic) bowl until dissolved. Microwave on high for 30 seconds if you need to help dissolve the sugar. Brush on top of the buns as soon as they come out of the oven.

You did it! Homemade hot cross buns! They won't look perfect because it's home baking and you can't produce buns like the bought ones — nor should you want to. No matter what they look like, you're an absolute legend and they will taste better to you than anything you've bought from a shop. They'll keep in an airtight bag or container for a few days, but if eating them more than half a day later, I'd toast them. Always serve with lashings of butter.

Dough-rising tips

♥ There's no set time for dough to rise. It will usually be fine at room temperature in the warmer months. It will rise slowly in cold conditions and faster in warm humid conditions (the ideal temperature is 22–27°C). If it's very cold, try placing a bowl or tray of just-boiled water in a turned-off oven and pop the covered dough in the oven with it. Shut the door and there will be enough warmth trapped in there to help it rise nicely. It's worth noting that yeast dies at temperatures above 60°C, so don't be tempted to warm it up too much.

Kneading tips

♥ Proper kneading at the start means a lighter bun at the end. Knead by pushing the dough — literally stretching it out — downward and away from you with the heel of your hand, then grabbing it and bringing it back on itself and repeating. You're stretching out the gluten strands in the flour so the dough can rise properly. At the end, try to gently stretch out a chunk of the dough as thin as possible with your fingers — when the dough is ready, it should stretch enough that you can see light through it. If it's not ready, it will just tear. You'll get there — just keep going until you do. It's a good workout!

Tips for using a machine

♥ You can use the dough hook on your cake mixer to start the kneading process. Use a low speed for 5 minutes. You'll need to finish the kneading by hand for another few minutes to get the 'see-through' result I've mentioned above, which is critical.

Nutty Apricot Balls

500g dried apricots, roughly chopped

1½ cups raw nuts (almonds, cashews, hazelnuts)

¾ cup desiccated coconut

¾ cup rolled oats

¾ cup ground linseed (flax seed)

⅓ cup cacao powder

1 tbsp chia seeds (optional)

½ tsp salt

———

PREP 15 MINUTES   **MAKES** ABOUT 20 BALLS

It's good to balance out the naughty treats with the good ones! To that end, these balls are my go-to. They'll help satisfy your sweet tooth, but with no added sugar. The nuts, oats and seeds in there add a bit of nutritional oomph, too. See if you can find dried apricots that are organic or haven't had any nitrates added to them — they will look ugly and brown instead of bright orange, which is a good thing. Cacao is different to cocoa powder in that it's raw — with plenty of health benefits. You should be able to find it in your supermarket nowadays, but if you can't normal cocoa is fine.

Place the chopped apricots in a medium saucepan with ¼ cup water. Cover with a lid and place over a medium heat. Simmer for 5–10 minutes until the apricots have soaked up the water. Keep an eye on them so they don't burn. Set aside to cool a little.

Put the remaining ingredients in a large food processor and blitz to a coarse crumb. Add the apricots and pulse again until combined — you may need to scrape down the sides a few times.

Roll into snack-sized balls and keep in an airtight container in the fridge to keep the nuts and seeds fresh.

Lemon Squeezy Slice

250g coconut biscuits, e.g. Krispie biscuits

250g wheat digestive biscuits

1 cup rolled oats

1 cup desiccated coconut

1 x 395g can sweetened condensed milk

125g butter, melted

zest of 4 medium lemons

1 tbsp lemon juice

½ tsp salt

Icing

1¾ cups icing sugar, sifted

75g butter, melted

2 tsp lemon juice

zest of 1 lemon

pinch salt

2 tsp just-boiled water

____

PREP 15 MINUTES PLUS A FEW HOURS SETTING TIME **MAKES** 15 SLICES

Easy peasy lemon squeezy is how we roll with this slice. It's got a real old-school vibe and it's 100 per cent awesome. There's no baking involved, it's quick to throw together and absolutely, addictively delicious. If you need to make it gluten-free, you can use your favourite gluten-free biscuits, and replace the oats with extra coconut and crumbled-up biscuits. It makes a lovely gift.

Line a 20cm x 20cm slice tin with baking paper so it goes up the sides.

Break up the biscuits into a food processor and process to a crumb. (Or, place biscuits in a ziplock bag and crush to a crumb with a rolling pin.)

Add the oats, coconut, condensed milk, butter, lemon zest, lemon juice and salt, and process again to combine. I find tilting the food processor helps keep the mixture turning. (If you don't have a food processor, place the crumb mixture in a mixing bowl with the oats, coconut, condensed milk, butter, lemon zest, lemon juice and salt. Stir to combine evenly.)

Press the crumb mixture firmly into the tin in an even layer.

To make the icing, put the icing sugar, melted butter, lemon juice and zest and salt in a bowl. Stir with a whisk.

Add teaspoons of the just-boiled water until it just comes together into a smooth thick-ish icing. Pour over the slice and spread out evenly. Cover and refrigerate for a few hours until set.

Cut into slices and keep in the fridge for a couple of weeks (that's a LOL right there!). It's fine out of the fridge, too, in an airtight container.

Fresh Ginger & Pear Loaf

200g butter, cubed

¾ cup brown sugar

⅓ cup golden syrup

1 tsp pure vanilla extract

½ cup milk

3 tbsp finely grated fresh ginger

1 free-range egg, at room
temperature

1 free-range egg yolk, at room
temperature

2 medium pears, peeled

2 cups plain flour

1 tbsp ground ginger

2 tsp baking powder

½ tsp baking soda

½ tsp ground cardamom

½ tsp salt

———

PREP 15 MINUTES **COOK** 1 HOUR 10 MINUTES **MAKES** 1 LOAF

When I was in San Fran last year, I went to the pier for a little look-see. I
ended up finding a funky restaurant and ordering dessert at three in the
afternoon, just because I could. It was an amazing pear loaf and instead of
being made with powdered ginger, it was fragrant and alive with the taste
of fresh ginger. It was soft, buttery and utterly divine, so I came home and
spent weeks trying to get it right. This is the result — it's pretty close! You
can either serve it as is, with butter, or as a dessert warm with ice cream
(and a little syrup and orange zest).

Preheat the oven to 150°C regular bake. Line a loaf tin (about 23cm x
10cm) with baking paper so it sticks up over the sides a few centimetres.

Place the butter, sugar, golden syrup and vanilla in a medium saucepan
and stir over a low heat until melted. Remove from the heat, leave to cool
for 10 minutes, then add the milk, fresh ginger, egg and yolk. Whisk to
combine.

Cut the pears into quarters and remove the cores. Thinly slice the pears.

Into a large mixing bowl sift the flour, ground ginger, baking powder,
baking soda, cardamom and salt. Stir to combine. Make a well in the
centre and add the butter mixture, stirring with a whisk to combine until
almost smooth — a few tiny lumps are okay.

Fold half the sliced pears through the loaf batter and scrape into the tin.
Arrange the remaining slices down each side of the tin, angled inwards a
bit, so the middle is exposed and can still rise.

Bake in the preheated oven for 1 hour 10 minutes, or until a skewer
inserted into the centre comes out clean. Cool in the tin for 15 minutes or
so, then turn out onto a cooling rack.

Keeps in an airtight container at room temperature for a few days.

Oat My Goodness Slice

Caramel filling

2 x 395g cans sweetened
    condensed milk (not lite)

150g butter

¼ cup brown sugar

2 tbsp golden syrup

Oaty goodness

250g butter, at room
    temperature, cubed

1 cup brown sugar, firmly packed

2 tsp vanilla essence

1½ cups plain flour

1 tsp baking powder

1½ cups rolled oats

¾ cup desiccated coconut

¼ tsp salt

———

PREP 20 MINUTES **COOK** 45 MINUTES **MAKES** 16–20 SLICES

One of my lovely Facebook fans named this slice for me, since the usual 'Oaty Caramel Slice' seemed like a bit of a yawn. And this is definitely not the usual! The name fits the bill perfectly because when you look at this slice, it really is a bit of an 'OMG' moment — and it tastes just heavenly. Will it be the most popular sweet recipe in this book? Time will tell . . .

Preheat the oven to 160°C regular bake. Line a 20cm square or 20cm x 30cm slice tin with baking paper so it fits nicely in the corners and goes up the sides all the way around — you may need two pieces.

To make the caramel, place the condensed milk, butter, brown sugar and golden syrup in a saucepan over medium-low heat. Stir continuously until only just melted and combined (no need to simmer or boil). Remove from the heat and set aside.

Cream the butter and sugar for a few minutes until pale and fluffy. Beat in the vanilla essence. Sift in the flour and baking powder, then add the oats, coconut and salt. Stir to combine — it will look a bit dry and crumbly.

Press two-thirds of the oat mixture into the base of the tin in an even layer (a layer of baking paper on top can help prevent sticking). Pour the caramel over the base.

Bake in the preheated oven for 15 minutes. Remove from the oven and let sit for 5 minutes until the caramel gets a skin on top.

Crumble the remaining oat mixture lightly over the caramel. Return to the oven for another 25–30 minutes. The edges of the caramel should be deep golden and puffy when it's ready, and the crumb starting to go golden all over.

Remove from the oven and allow to cool in the tin, then refrigerate before slicing to allow the caramel to set. I reckon it's best stored in the fridge, too, where it will keep for about a week.

Cookies & Cream Dream

Base

350g chocolate cookies (a
    chocolate cookie preferably
    with choc chips in it)

100g butter, softened

½ cup rolled oats

3 tbsp cocoa or cacao powder

1 tsp pure vanilla extract or paste

pinch salt

Cookies & cream filling

200g butter, at room
    temperature, cubed

250g cream cheese, at room
    temperature

125g good-quality white
    chocolate, chopped

3 tbsp cream

2½ cups icing sugar

1 tbsp cornflour

1 tsp pure vanilla extract or paste

¼ tsp salt

¾ cup finely chopped dark
    chocolate

Chocolate topping

150g good-quality dark chocolate
    (at least 50% cocoa solids),
    chopped

1 tbsp olive oil

PREP 30 MINUTES PLUS 4+ HOURS SETTING TIME
MAKES ABOUT 20 PIECES

Okay, so this slice is a little bit outrageous — I think it's the equivalent of the Snickalicious Slice from *Scrumptious*, actually. Which means it's going to be a popular one because you guys are just so naughty. It's creamy and sweet, as it should be — so you only need little slices. This was Mike's favourite of all the sweets in this book — excitement always ensued after dinner when he realised there was a container of it in the fridge. He'd have this and I'd have the Chocolate Orange Sherbet Slice on page 182.

Remove the butter and cream cheese for the filling from the fridge 30 minutes or so before you start so they can come to room temperature. If you're rushed for time, you can microwave each separately on a low heat for 20 seconds or so.

Line the base and sides of a 20cm x 20cm (or near enough) slice tin with baking paper.

Crumble the cookies up into a food processor and add the butter, rolled oats, cocoa or cacao, vanilla and salt. Process to a very fine crumb, then tip into the prepared tin and press firmly into an even layer.

Put the chopped white chocolate and cream in a ceramic or glass mixing bowl and microwave on high for 1 minute. Stir until smooth. You can microwave for another 30 seconds if it needs it. Set aside.

Beat the butter in a large mixing bowl on medium speed for a couple of minutes until pale and fluffy. Add the cream cheese and beat again until well combined. Sift in the icing sugar and cornflour, add the vanilla and salt and beat until smooth.

Scrape the melted chocolate and cream into the cream cheese mixture and stir or beat on a low speed until smooth, scraping the sides of the bowl as you go.

Fold the chopped dark chocolate through the mixture until combined.

Scrape the mixture out on top of the base, smooth with a spatula or the back of a warmed spoon, cover and refrigerate for at least 4 hours or overnight.

You can add the icing after the base has firmed up in the fridge for at least an hour. Microwave the chocolate in the same way you did for the filling above. Stir in the oil and spread on top of the filling with the back of a spoon. Refrigerate again until set.

Slice into pieces when it's well chilled, then keep the slices in an airtight container in the fridge for up to a week. It will soften quite a bit in warm weather if it's out of the fridge.

Coffee Cake

Cake

5 tbsp instant coffee dissolved in 1 cup just-boiled water

3 cups plain flour

3 tsp baking powder

1 tsp fine sea salt

½ tsp baking soda

2 cups caster sugar

2 free-range eggs

¾ cup milk

200g butter, melted

3 tsp pure vanilla extract

Icing

100g butter, softened

2½ cups icing sugar

2 tbsp instant coffee dissolved in 2 tbsp just-boiled water and left to cool

pinch salt

cocoa, for dusting

___

PREP 15 MINUTES **COOK** 1 HOUR **SERVES** 8–10

Back in the day, before double-shot lattes and Frappuccinos took over the country, coffee was a humbler affair (instant, baby!). This cake is a nod to those days. It reminds me of instant coffee with sweetened condensed milk added to it — gorgeously sweet and decadent. The icing is just ridiculously tasty. This is a big cake — if your tin isn't large enough, it might overflow in the oven.

Preheat the oven to 160°C regular bake and set a rack just below the centre of the oven. Line the base of a 24–25cm round springform tin with baking paper, and grease the sides (you can paper the sides, too, if it's an old tin).

Prepare the coffee mixture and leave to cool to warm.

Sift the flour, baking powder, salt and baking soda into a large mixing bowl.

Place the sugar, eggs, milk, melted butter, vanilla and cooled coffee mixture in a separate medium-sized mixing bowl. Beat lightly with a whisk for a minute or so until the sugar is mostly dissolved.

Make a large well in the dry ingredients and pour the wet mixture in. Using the whisk, stir in a circular motion from the middle until the dry mixture is incorporated into the wet, with no big lumps. You don't have to be gentle here, but don't actually whisk the mixture. Scrape the mixture into the prepared tin.

Bake in the preheated oven for 1 hour, or until a skewer inserted into the centre comes out clean. Leave to cool for 10 minutes in the tin, then turn out onto a wire rack to cool. Keeps for a couple of days in an airtight container.

Icing

To make the icing, place the butter in a mixing bowl with the icing sugar, cooled coffee mixture and salt. Beat for 1–2 minutes until smooth, light and fluffy. Ice the cake when it's completely cool with a small spatula or a warm knife. Dust with cocoa.

Tuck Shop Donuts

2 cups plain flour

½ cup high-grade flour

2 tbsp sugar, plus ½ tsp to activate the yeast

¼ tsp salt

⅓ cup warm water

1½ tsp active dried yeast (check the expiry date)

25g chilled butter, finely chopped

½ cup milk

1 free-range egg, lightly beaten

approx. 1 litre neutral oil, e.g. grapeseed, for frying

To serve

½ cup icing sugar

1¼ cups cream, whipped with ¼ cup icing sugar

raspberry or strawberry jam, to garnish

———

Chelsea's tips

♥ Keep the leftover cream-filled donuts in an airtight container in the fridge (and good luck with that). Unfilled ones can stay at room temperature in an airtight container for a day.

♥ If you want to be truly truly truly outrageous, you can fold half custard and half whipped cream together and use this to fill the donuts.

♥ You can roll the dough into balls for round donuts, if you like.

PREP 15 MINUTES PLUS 3–5 HOURS RISING TIME   **COOK** 10 MINUTES
MAKES 8 DONUTS

Behold the glorious, old-school donut! So many of you have asked me for a good donut recipe. And finally, five books in, here it is. I'm obviously a huge donut fan (who isn't), but my tastes are rather simple — I get misty-eyed with nostalgia when I think about the donuts that used to come in that paper bag, delivered to the classroom in a big plastic bin at lunchtime by the tuck shop lady. Frankfurter roll shape + whipped cream + icing sugar + stingy dollop of jam. Sweet, soft, sticky-fingered bliss. We no longer have to be stingy with the jam, though!

Place the flours, 2 tablespoons of sugar, and salt in a large mixing bowl (metal or plastic is good) and stir to combine.

Pour the water into a mug with ½ teaspoon of sugar and stir briskly. Sprinkle the yeast over the top. Let sit for 30 seconds, then whisk with a fork for 20 seconds. If you're using 'instant' yeast (check the label), go straight to the next step. For active dry yeast, wait 5–10 minutes for the yeast to go frothy on top.

Stir the yeast mixture again to swish up any solids sitting on the bottom, then add to the flour mixture along with the butter, milk and egg. Use a fork to stir the mixture until it forms a rough dough.

Lightly flour a clean benchtop and tip the dough out on to it (scrape out the bowl, too). It may feel very sticky at the moment — dust your hands lightly with flour and start to knead it. Rub the dough off your hands as you go, and scrape any stubborn dough from the bench with a blunt spatula or scraper. You can add a little more flour if needed, though resist the temptation to add too much — a sticky dough is good. As you keep kneading, it will lose its stickiness.

When it's more solid, knead for about 5–10 minutes until it's lovely and smooth, soft and elastic.

Place the dough back in the mixing bowl, and cover by fitting a plastic supermarket bag on top. Leave the dough in a draught-free place until it has doubled in size. There's no set time for this to happen — it could be 1–2 hours. In summer it will happen quicker than winter. If it's very cold you could pop the bowl in the turned-off oven above a small tray of just-boiled water. Don't be tempted to put it close to something hot, because temperatures 60°C and over actually kill the yeast.

When doubled in size, scrape the dough out onto the benchtop (I try to do it with no flour). Divide the dough in eight even pieces, then roll each piece out into a fat log shape.

Recipe continued over page . . .

Line a large oven tray (or two trays) with baking paper, and brush with some of the oil. Arrange the dough logs on the tray/s with enough space between them to double in size without touching. Cover with a lightly oiled piece of cling wrap and leave to rest again in a draught-free place until they have doubled in size.

Add enough oil to a medium-large saucepan to half fill it. Place over a medium-low heat and let the oil temperature reach about 180°C. If you don't have a cooking thermometer, dip in the end of a wooden spoon to test. Bubbles will start to fizz around the end when the oil is ready. (Never leave hot oil unattended.)

Set up a wire rack with paper towels or newspaper underneath for the cooked donuts.

Now cook the doughnuts — probably two at a time. You don't want to squish them, so the best way to transfer them to the oil is to cut the baking paper around each one with scissors or a knife, then lift each log off the tray separately, and gently ease it off the paper into the oil — don't splash hot oil on yourself.

Cook the donuts for a couple of minutes, carefully turning once, until they are a deep golden brown on each side.

Transfer the doughnuts to the rack and immediately dust them generously with icing sugar, so the oil on the outside soaks it up. Leave to cool.

To serve, slice longways from the top almost all the way through. Fill with whipped cream, then smear with jam.

These donuts are best eaten the day you make them — preferably while slightly warm! Because they're homemade with no additives or preservatives to keep them soft, they don't last long — that's just the way it goes.

Apricot Yoghurt Loaf

1 free-range egg

1 free-range egg yolk

1¾ cups chopped dried apricots

1⅓ cups water

175g butter, at room
temperature, cubed

1½ cups brown sugar

2 tsp vanilla essence

2 cups plain flour

2½ tsp baking powder

¼ tsp salt

¾ cup plain unsweetened
yoghurt (or milk)

——

Chelsea's tips

♥ Don't fret if your loaf sinks
slightly in the middle — this
is quite common because the
deep sides of a loaf tin cause
the outside to cook more quickly
than the inside.

PREP 25 MINUTES **COOK** 1 HOUR 20 MINUTES
MAKES 1 LARGE LOAF

There's something incredibly comforting about a good old-fashioned
apricot loaf. I was very picky when testing this recipe — it needed to be
soft, not dry but not too squidgy, able to take a good spread of butter
and have lots of yummy apricots. And by hokey, it's perfect! The oven
temperature might seem quite low, but for some reason this loaf just
wanted it, so who am I to argue? It takes a little longer but ensures even
cooking and less sinkage in the middle.

Remove the eggs from the fridge to come to room temperature.

Preheat the oven to 150°C regular bake. Line a loaf tin (about 23cm x
10cm) with baking paper so it sticks up over the sides a few centimetres.

Place the chopped apricots and water in a medium saucepan over a
medium-low heat. Cover with a lid and allow to simmer for about
20 minutes, stirring occasionally — all the water should soak into the
apricots and they should go nice and mushy. Watch that they don't burn.
Transfer to a dinner plate, spread out so they cool quicker and place in
the fridge.

Cream the butter and sugar in a cake mixer or with an electric beater for
a few minutes until pale and fluffy. Add the egg and yolk, and beat for
another minute. Add the vanilla essence and beat briefly to combine.

Sift the flour, baking powder and salt into a medium bowl and stir to
combine evenly.

Add half the flour mixture to the creamed mixture and gently fold to
combine. Add the yoghurt (or milk), fold again to combine, then add the
remaining flour. Lastly fold in the cooled apricots. Scrape the mixture into
the prepared tin.

Bake in the preheated oven for 1 hour and 20 minutes, or until a skewer
poked in comes out clean. Cool in the tin for 10 minutes.

Remove the loaf from the tin and set on a wire rack to cool completely
before slicing. I prefer the texture of the loaf the next day — so when it's
cool, I wrap it up and leave it overnight. It's easier to slice and the crust is
softer. Lovely with a wee spread of butter.

Keeps in an airtight container at room temperature for a few days.

Cranberry & White Choc Fridge Fudge

500g good-quality white
    chocolate

100ml cream

50g butter, chopped

1 cup dried cranberries

1 cup chopped Brazil nuts (or nut
    of your choice)

zest of 1 large lemon

1 tbsp lemon juice

1 tsp flaky sea salt

———

PREP 10 MINUTES PLUS 4 HOURS SETTING TIME
MAKES ABOUT 20 SQUARES

I suppose this isn't really a fudge, because it doesn't involve cooking sugar and all that jazz — it's far easier to make and looks rather impressive. I call it fridge fudge because when it's kept in the fridge (or the freezer), it firms up and turns all chewy and delicious.

Line a 20cm square slice tin with baking paper so it goes up the sides.

Chop the chocolate up and put in a microwave-proof (glass or ceramic) bowl with the cream. Microwave on high for 1 minute, stir well with a wooden spoon, then microwave on high again for 40 seconds. Stir until the chocolate is melted. Add the butter in three lots, stirring well between each addition until completely incorporated.

Stir through the cranberries, nuts, lemon zest, lemon juice and salt. Scrape into the prepared tin, sprinkle with extra cranberries/nuts if you like, cover and refrigerate for at least 4 hours or overnight, until set.

Slice into squares and keep in an airtight container in the fridge for a week.

Trickery Ice Cream

600ml cream (or use heavy/double cream if you can find it)

1 x 395g can sweetened condensed milk

1 tsp pure vanilla extract or paste

—

Chelsea's tips

♥ If you're not fussed on presentation, you can use an old ice cream container or a plastic container with a lid to freeze the ice cream in.

PREP 15 MINUTES PLUS 7+ HOURS SETTING TIME   **SERVES** 8

Looks like ice cream, tastes like ice cream — but you can make it at home without an ice cream maker and without making custard so, technically, it's not reeeeally ice cream. Your guests will be hoodwinked! But damn, it is really good! I can't take credit for the overall concept as it was someone else's idea. However, I've added my own Kiwi flavour twists here; especially with the mint chocolate chip. Oh, lord it's good!

In a large mixing bowl, beat the cream, condensed milk and vanilla with an electric beater on a medium speed for a couple of minutes until you have a beautiful light airy mixture. Scrape into a loaf tin.

Cover tightly with cling wrap, then a layer of foil — you don't want any freezer air getting in and tainting it. Freeze for at least 7 hours or overnight.

Remove from the freezer 10 minutes before serving. Scoop it out with an ice cream scoop or soup spoon that you've warmed in a mug of very hot/just-boiled water.

Mint choc chip ice cream

Omit the vanilla and fold 2½ teaspoons peppermint essence and 1 cup finely chopped milk chocolate into the whipped ice cream mixture before transferring to the loaf tin. Or, if you want to really take it to the next level, add chopped after dinner mints instead of chocolate.

Coffee & walnut ice cream

Dissolve 2½ tablespoons instant coffee in 2 tablespoons just-boiled water in a mug. Refrigerate to cool completely, then fold through the whipped ice cream mixture along with ¾ cup chopped fresh walnuts before transferring to the loaf tin. You could use pecans instead of walnuts.

Lemon & feijoa ice cream

Omit the vanilla and fold as much chopped feijoa as you like (around ¾ cup is good), 1 tablespoon lemon juice and some lemon zest into the whipped ice cream mixture before transferring to the loaf tin.

Chocolate Hazelnut Cheesecake

Base

1 cup hazelnuts

250g plain biscuits (digestives are nice), roughly broken

150g very soft butter

⅓ cup rolled oats

2 tbsp cocoa or cacao powder

1 tsp vanilla essence

¼ tsp salt

Filling

500g cream cheese

1 cup chocolate hazelnut spread (one that doesn't contain palm oil)

1½ cups cream

Topping

¾ cup cream, whipped

⅓ cup chopped dark chocolate

———

Chelsea's tips

♥ Keeps in an airtight container in the fridge for about 5 days.

♥ It can also be frozen in the tin if very airtight — wrap in a double layer of foil and then a double layer of cling wrap, and freeze for up to 3 months.

PREP 30 MINUTES PLUS 6+ HOURS SETTING TIME   **SERVES** 8–10

I have a funny feeling a lot of people are going to be *very* excited about this recipe. Hell, I'm excited about it — look at it! And I love that it's so super easy to make — you don't have to faff around with baking the filling (well, you quickly roast the hazelnuts, but that's not a major). I'm a big believer in rejecting products that contain palm oil, so I'd recommend you check the chocolate hazelnut spread labels — you'll be doing the orangutans and our other rainforest friends a favour.

Remove the cream cheese from the fridge 30 minutes or so prior to making the cheesecake if you can; otherwise warm for 10–20 seconds on medium power in the microwave in a glass or ceramic mixing bowl.

Preheat the oven to 180°C regular bake (just for roasting the hazelnuts).

Line the base of a 24–25cm round cake tin with baking paper and very lightly grease the sides with butter.

Place the hazelnuts in a small roasting tray and roast in the preheated oven for 8–10 minutes until golden and fragrant. Tip into a clean tea towel (use an old one as it may stain brown) and fold up the corners. Massage/rub vigorously until most of the brown skins have come away from the nuts. Don't be too fussy here, though; a bit of skin is fine.

Set aside one-third of the hazelnuts for the topping. Place the other two-thirds in a food processor with the other base ingredients and process to a fine crumb. Tip into the prepared tin and press down firmly in an even layer. Set aside.

In a large mixing bowl, beat the cream cheese on a medium speed for 30 seconds or so until smooth (or you can beat by hand). Add the chocolate hazelnut spread and beat on a low speed to just combine evenly.

Whip the cream to soft, billowy peaks in a medium mixing bowl (be careful not to overwhip or it will go lumpy and grainy — if it does, stir in a few tablespoons of runny cream by hand with a whisk). Add the whipped cream to the cream cheese mixture and fold gently until combined evenly. Scrape on top of the prepared base and smooth out with a spatula. Cover and refrigerate for at least 6 hours or overnight.

Just before serving, **cover with a layer of whipped cream and sprinkle with** the remaining chopped toasted hazelnuts and chopped chocolate. You can also dust with cocoa and icing sugar if you want to go all out.

Apple Puffs

3 large apples, peeled
2 tbsp brown sugar
2 tbsp sugar
2 tbsp custard powder
1 tsp ground cinnamon
pinch salt
3 sheets flaky puff pastry
50g butter, chopped into small pieces
1 free-range egg, beaten with 1 tbsp milk (egg wash)

——

PREP 15 MINUTES **COOK** 30 MINUTES **SERVES** 6

These are my answer to apple turnovers — they're quick and easier to make than turnovers because there's no actual pastry turning-over involved! There's a good chance you always have a few sheets of pastry in the freezer and apples in the fruit bowl — so this may become a favourite year-round treat you can whip up whenever you have a hankering. Served warm with ice cream they're pretty damn good — but they're also just as awesome cold the next day.

Preheat the oven to 180°C fan-bake and set a rack in the centre of the oven. Line a large baking tray with baking paper.

Slice the apples very thinly.

Place the brown sugar, sugar, custard powder, cinnamon and salt in a bowl and stir with a fork to combine.

Cut each pastry sheet into four even squares. Place apple slices in the middle of one square, as many as will comfortably fit, leaving a 1cm edge clear. Sprinkle a teaspoon of the sugary mixture over the apples, and top with a few bits of butter. Lay another square of pastry carefully on top and press down firmly all along the edges to seal. Repeat with the remaining pastry squares — you might not use up all the sugar mixture.

Brush the pastry tops with the egg wash, let sit for a minute, then cut a few steam holes in the tops. Place on the lined tray.

Bake in the preheated oven for 30 minutes until golden-brown all over and puffy.

Allow to cool for about 5 minutes (the filling will be really hot), then serve with cream and ice cream (see page 216).

Raspberry, Yoghurt & White Chocolate Cups

1½ cups thick Greek yoghurt, plus extra to serve

500g fresh (or frozen) raspberries (defrosted)

150g white chocolate, chopped

¾ cup cream, plus 2 tbsp

1 tbsp lemon juice

1–2 punnets fresh berries to serve (optional)

———

PREP 30 MINUTES PLUS 4+ HOURS SETTING TIME **SERVES** 6

This is a light, fresh dessert that isn't too sweet — the yoghurt and fresh raspberries cut through the white chocolate lusciousness rather nicely. It's not quite a mousse, not quite a pudding — it's just a delicious chilled berry dessert thing that everyone will love. What more could you ask for, really? If fresh raspberries aren't in season, you can just use defrosted whole berries for the top instead.

Remove the yoghurt from the fridge 30 minutes before you make the mousse — it needs to come to room temperature. You could also microwave for 20 seconds on medium-low in a microwave-proof (glass or ceramic) bowl.

Blitz the berries in a food processor until smooth. Press/scrape the mixture through a sieve into a mixing bowl using a bendy spatula. Discard the seeds and dry pulp at the end. Set the berry purée aside.

Place the white chocolate and ¼ cup cream in a medium-sized microwave-proof (glass or ceramic) bowl, and microwave uncovered for 60 seconds on high. Stir in a circular motion until smooth — you can microwave again for 30 seconds if it needs it. Add the 2 tbsp cream and stir again to combine.

Add the yoghurt to the white chocolate mixture, a spoonful at a time to start with, stirring gently until combined evenly. Fold through the berry purée.

Whip the remaining ½ cup cream. Add to the yoghurt mixture and fold to combine. Fold through the lemon juice.

If you like, you can also fold through a few fresh berries now. Spoon or pour the mixture into serving glasses or bowls or ramekins, cover and refrigerate for at least 4 hours to set.

When ready to serve, dollop a spoonful of fresh yoghurt on the top and finish with a few fresh berries. If you can find freeze-dried berries, they are nice as a garnish, too.

Chocolate Crack Topping

200g good-quality dark eating chocolate

¼ cup virgin coconut oil

ice cream, to serve (see page 216)

———

Chelsea's tips

♥ I always used to like the mint choc version — to that end, you could add a teaspoon of peppermint essence to this mixture if you like.

PREP 10 MINUTES   **MAKES** ENOUGH FOR ABOUT 15 SERVES

If this doesn't remind you of your childhood, then I'll be a monkey's uncle. My version, of course, is a vast improvement, as it's homemade and without all the added nasties. You'll be amazed at how simple and effective the recipe is. Your kids (and big kids) are gonna love it. Get those spoons and start smashing!

Chop up the chocolate and place in a large microwave-proof (glass or ceramic) bowl. Microwave on high for 1 minute 20 seconds. Stir to combine. It should be melted — if not, put it back in for another 30 seconds on high.

Stir through the coconut oil to combine evenly.

Drizzle on top of your ice cream, wait 30 seconds or so for it to harden — then you will be able to crack it with the back of a spoon.

Store the topping in an airtight glass jar or bottle in a dark place for up to 6 months. It may be solid when you go to use it — just zap it in the microwave for 30–40 seconds on high to bring it back. Make sure the jar or container is microwave-proof, and remove the lid before microwaving.

Custardy Hot Cross Pudding

6–9 hot cross buns

75g butter, softened

¾ cup chopped dark chocolate
(optional)

2 cups milk

1 cup cream

2 free-range eggs

¼ cup brown sugar

3 tbsp custard powder dissolved
in 3 tbsp water or milk

2 tsp vanilla essence

½ tsp ground cinnamon

½ tsp salt

____

PREP 7 MINUTES **COOK** 30 MINUTES **SERVES** 4–6

Whether you buy them or make your own (see page 190), it's hard not to
be buried in an avalanche of hot cross buns at Easter time. You may enjoy
a new way to use them other than being a toasted vehicle for a truckload
of butter (yum). This is a wonderful way to use up slightly stale buns and
provide a simple, delicious pudding to a hungry crowd. Choose the buns
you like; with or without fruit or peel — or with added chocolate for you
naughty ones.

Preheat the oven to 180°C regular bake. Grease a medium-sized baking
dish.

Slice the hot cross buns in half and generously butter each side — use
all the butter up. Tear or break the halves into another 2–3 pieces, and
arrange in the baking dish. Scatter with the chocolate, if using.

In a medium saucepan off the heat, whisk the milk, cream, eggs, sugar,
custard powder mixture, vanilla essence, cinnamon and salt to combine to
a smooth mixture (you don't need it to get foamy).

Set over a medium heat on the stovetop, and stir constantly until it only
just starts to thicken — you don't want it to turn into a thick custard yet;
it just needs to come together enough so it doesn't separate while baking.
Pour all over the hot cross bun pieces.

Bake in the preheated oven for 30 minutes until the tops are crunchy and
the middle is soft and custardy.

Serve with ice cream and runny or whipped cream.

Custard Fruit Tarts

3–4 sheets sweet short pastry, defrosted

fresh seasonal fruit (e.g. berries, mandarin segments, grapes, passionfruit, sliced orange, pineapple, kiwifruit)

icing sugar, for dusting

Custard

2 cups milk

2 cups cream

2 free-range eggs

½ cup sugar

5 tbsp custard powder mixed with 3 tbsp milk

zest of 2 oranges

pinch salt

—

Chelsea's tips

♥ You can melt some inexpensive apricot jam for topping instead of the icing sugar if you like — just heat in a mug in the microwave for 40 seconds and brush on the tarts for a nice gloss.

♥ Leftover custard is delicious with fruit for dessert — it keeps for a few days in the fridge.

PREP 35 MINUTES **COOK** 15 MINUTES **MAKES** 12–16 TARTS

You fruity little tart, you! Isn't this photo just outrageously beautiful? These tarts aren't hard to make and the custard is seriously delicious — super creamy with a delightful hint of orange. Decorate your little tarts with whatever fresh fruit is in season and what you like to eat.

Preheat the oven to 180°C regular bake and set a rack in the centre of the oven. Grease a 12-pan muffin tray with butter. Cut a little circle or square of baking paper to fit on the bottom of each pan — it doesn't have to be a perfect fit.

Use a round pastry cutter about 9cm in diameter (or use a bowl or mug about that size and cut around it) and cut out 4–5 rounds per pastry sheet. Gently press each pastry circle down into the tray and prick with a fork.

Cut circles of baking paper to fit each hole, so they come all the way up past the sides of the pastry. Press gently into the holes. Fill each cup with uncooked rice, lentils or baking beads.

Bake in the preheated oven for 10 minutes, then carefully pull out the paper cases and rice — and carefully remove any rice that has spilled on the pastry. Be gentle, as the paper can stick.

Bake the naked pastry cases again for 5–8 minutes until just turning light golden. Remove from the tray before they cool completely, or they can stick to the sides and become hard to remove. Peel the paper off the bottoms.

To make the custard, pour the milk and cream into a medium saucepan and place over a medium heat. Watch it like a hawk — as soon as it gets too hot to leave your finger in for a few seconds, remove it from the heat (little bubbles will have started forming around the edges, too).

Whisk the eggs in a large mixing bowl with the sugar and custard powder mixture. Add ¼ cup of the hot milk mixture to the beaten eggs, whisking all the time as you add it (this gets the eggs used to the heat so they don't curdle). Pour in the rest of the hot milk and stir.

Give the milk pot a quick rinse and scrub, place a sieve over it and pour the milky egg mixture back in. Add the orange zest and salt. Replace over a medium heat and stir continuously with a whisk for about 5 minutes until it's nice and thick. Remove from the heat and cover with cling wrap to stop a skin forming (or sprinkle the surface with a little sugar). Leave to cool — you can refrigerate if you like.

Spoon the custard into the pastry cases, right to the top. Top with fruit and dust with icing sugar.

I keep my assembled tarts in an airtight container in the fridge — they are fine for a couple of days.

— pantry talk
—

Staples

Sauces, vinegars, condiments and flavour heroes

Anchovies
Balsamic vinegar
Beef stock (liquid)
Capers
Chicken stock (liquid)
Dijon mustard
Fish stock (liquid)
Malt vinegar
Oils (see page 232)
Peppercorns in a grinder
Red or white wine vinegar
Salt (see right)
Soy sauce (naturally brewed)
Sweet Thai chilli sauce
Tabasco or chilli sauce
Thai fish sauce
Tomato paste
White vinegar
Worcestershire sauce

Canned

Cannellini beans
Chickpeas
Coconut cream
Coconut milk
Sweetened condensed milk
Tomatoes

Spice drawer

Allspice
Cardamom
Chilli flakes or powder
Chinese five-spice
Cinnamon
Cloves
Coriander
Cumin (ground)
Cumin seeds
Curry powder
Finely ground black pepper
Finely ground white pepper
Garam masala
Ginger
Mixed spice
Nutmeg
Oregano (dried)
Paprika
Sesame seeds
Star anise (whole)
Turmeric

Fresh herbs

You'll notice that I mostly use fresh herbs in my recipes. I grow lots of herbs in my garden and I enjoy picking them fresh. But if you only have dried herbs on hand, you can substitute one-third of the fresh amount for dried — or substitute another similar fresh herb.

I can't encourage you enough to grow some fresh herbs in a few pots outside or in a patch in the garden. Some fresh herbs that are really easy to grow and maintain are:

- ♥ Basil
- ♥ Bay tree (fresh bay leaves are the bomb!)
- ♥ Mint
- ♥ Oregano
- ♥ Parsley
- ♥ Rosemary
- ♥ Sage
- ♥ Thyme

Salt and oil

Salt

In New Zealand our soil is naturally very low in iodine, meaning our locally grown produce doesn't provide enough of it to satisfy our dietary requirements. The addition of iodine to our salt was a simple solution — personally, I always have some form of iodised salt on hand to use each day in conjunction with other, less-processed salts.

Here's a bit of a breakdown.

Iodised sea salt — This salt has had iodine added to it, but the salt itself is evaporated naturally from seawater so it retains many other minerals (albeit in very trace amounts). You can buy it in rock salt form and put it in your salt grinder, and also in flaky form which is great for serving on the table with food.

Iodised free-flowing table salt — This salt is usually purely sodium chloride (no other natural minerals) and contains additives to stop it clumping up. I normally use this salt when I need a good amount but it's not going to be seen — cooking water for potatoes, vegetables and pasta, and in soups, sauces and casseroles, etc.

Other natural specialty salts (Himalayan salt, Celtic sea salt, etc.) — The colour and flavour of these beautiful natural salts (of which there are many varieties) differ depending on what part of the world they come from — I'd encourage you to explore and have fun with them! I use these in little bowls on the table and the bench, for serving and sprinkling straight onto food.

Olive oil

This is a very important subject for me; I've learned a fascinating amount about olive oil from my travels in Italy and Spain. I think home cooks should be well informed about it, too — and the truth below might surprise you!

Extra virgin olive oil (EVOO for short) is a beautiful thing, very good for you and I would argue the only olive oil worth buying. I encourage you to use and consume it generously where it works with the flavours.

'Extra virgin' indicates that the oil has been extracted from the olives using mechanical methods (rather than heat or chemicals), so the oil retains the flavour, aroma and full nutritional value of the olives. The health benefits of EVOO are many.

In Europe, the simple rule is 'old wine, new oil'. EVOO doesn't keep well — it turns rancid very quickly when exposed to light and air so the fresher it is, the better. This means for us in New Zealand, a local EVOO might be the best choice (we have some lovely ones). Look for it in dark green bottles or even boxes in foil bladders — clear bottles are simply no good.

Olive oil that hasn't been specifically labelled as 'extra virgin' is oil that has been extracted from (probably low-grade) olives using chemicals and heat. Just because it comes from Europe doesn't mean it's quality. It's not something I would ever recommend you buy.

Light olive oil certainly doesn't mean light in fat (or calories, if that's your thing). It's made up of refined olive oil blended with other (cheaper) refined oils to make it lighter in colour and flavour, and so it can withstand higher cooking temperatures. I steer well clear of this one.

Other oils

Butter, grapeseed oil, peanut oil, sesame oil, coconut oil and avocado oil are always on hand in my kitchen. Which one you use depends on what kind of flavours you're cooking with in a geographical sense. If you're unsure, just use your noggin (for example, if it's an Indian-style curry, using avocado or sesame oil doesn't really make sense with the flavours).

Throughout this book, I've stated using grapeseed oil as a default for most of the pan-frying, browning and shallowing-frying, because it doesn't impart any flavour or colour to the final dish. You can use rice bran oil if you like, too.

Storing things

A few pointers for storing some of the more common ingredients.

Butter — Butter will turn rancid very quickly if left exposed to air and warmth. Store your butter in an airtight container in the fridge. It will pick up all the flavours from the fridge if not sealed properly. Scrape off and discard that dark yellow layer you sometimes see on the outside. I keep a small dish of soft butter on the bench for spreading purposes which I cut fresh from the block each day (you can also use a butter bell). As for margarine and other such spreads — I simply don't eat them.

Cheese — Once opened, blocks of cheese like being wrapped up individually in baking paper, and stored together in an airtight plastic container in the fridge. Parmesan should be stored separately.

Eggs — Eggs are best stored inside their original cardboard cartons on the middle shelf in the fridge (ironically, not in the egg holders in the fridge door).

Flour — Flour is best kept in a cool dark place. It contains oils which can eventually go rancid when exposed to light and warmth.

Fresh ginger — Keep in an airtight container or resealable bag in the vegetable drawer. Pat the cut end dry before storing.

Garlic — Unpeeled garlic bulbs should be stored as for potatoes, in a dry, dark place. Once peeled, the cloves keep in the fridge in an airtight container for a day or so. Side note — fresh New Zealand-grown garlic is best. I also think using pre-crushed or peeled garlic from a jar is to be avoided.

Nuts and seeds — In the warmer months, nuts and seeds are best kept in the fridge in an airtight container — this can be awkward if you don't have much room in the fridge, though. Buy them as you need them so you don't have to keep them too long.

Oils — Always store your oils in an airtight bottle or container in a dark, cool place. Light and air cause oils to turn rancid very quickly. A sealed, dark glass bottle (or tin) in a cupboard or drawer is best.

Potatoes, kumara, onions — Store in a dry, dark place in something made of natural fibre that allows air circulation — like a paper bag, cardboard box with holes punched in it or string bag. Plastic bags are a no-go. If your kumara starts to sprout, you can pop it in a jar of water and let it turn into a charming house plant, like I do.

Spices — Spices and herbs should be kept in airtight containers and stored in a dark, cool place to keep fresh and flavoursome. (And, sadly, scrunching the spice bag back down into the box doesn't count as airtight!). Little glass jars with a screw cap or a rubber seal clip-top are great.

A word about fridges and containers

Anything left in the fridge without being properly sealed will pick up all the other flavours from the fridge, dry out and taste real bad, real quick. I am by nature a 'slap dash' person and would love to be able to just chuck an uncovered plate of food in the fridge; but I care about the quality of my food, so I don't! To this end, plastic or glass containers with tight-fitting lids are great — they may cost a little more initially, but you can use them over and over meaning you're not continually throwing away loads of cling wrap, foil and disposable plastic containers.

Taking better care of our planet (as it's the only one we've got)

We're living in a time when we are creating a *lot* of unnecessary waste. It's quite scary, especially if you consider that more than 350,000 new people are being born in the world each day. If we all make some changes to our daily goings-on (beyond the weekly recycling bin), we can help make a difference. I'm by no means a perfect example. I'm still learning, but over the past couple of years I've realised how much I care about the state of the world that we're passing on to our children.

Here's what I'm doing. It's simple stuff — it's the sticking with it that requires the effort!

♥ I try to take reusable bags to the shops or use boxes for my groceries. I've found biodegradable poop-bags for Sprite the dog. I have a reusable glass water bottle (throw-away plastic water bottles are very bad for both you *and* the planet, believe me).

♥ Although we live in the city at the moment, I'm the proud owner of a nifty compost bin, which is also a worm farm — and I use the delicious juice from the worms to fertilise my house plants. It's an awesome feeling to know that my food scraps are on their way to becoming precious soil and ready to grow the next generation of plants.

♥ I try to use cling wrap very sparingly. There are other awesome options out there, like beeswax-coated cloths which are great for covering food. Sometimes baking paper will do the job. Or else, resealable airtight glass or plastic containers are a good option for storing food.

♥ I always choose free-range animal products if possible. Especially eggs. For me, this is important.

♥ And finally, to counter the 'throw-away' mentality that's rife in our society, I try not to buy things just for the sake of it — because they're on sale, in fashion, or because advertising tells me I 'need' them. I'm finding being content with what I have is much more fulfilling than wanting more 'stuff'. It's people and experiences (like eating delicious food) that offer true happiness. As a friend of mine wisely said, 'When we stop looking for happiness in material things, we find more of it in ourselves.'

I still have a long way to go, but it's a nice journey to be on. If you have any advice or insights, feel free to contact me, I'd love to hear from you!

Be the change you wish to see in the world. Be generous with your love, be conscious, and live from your heart.

thanks

My heart is full of gratitude for all the wonderful people who have helped me bring this book into being. In no particular order, **thank you** . . .

The sensational team at **Penguin Random House** — the heroic effort you all put in behind the scenes is not lost on me.

Tam West — You are one in a million. Your sensitivity, integrity and gentle dedication to true beauty is unique and infectious, and it radiates out of every page of this book. **Victoria Bell** — you're a delightful human being. Thank you for your intuitiveness and quiet brilliance. **Helen Gilligan-Reid** — your design talents are superb; and *Eat* looks superb.

Tony Price — for your energy and skill, and for putting bowls on your head and dancing around the kitchen burning doohoo sticks. Thanks to **Greasy McGibbon** for helping me make the best bolar roasts.

Mandy Scott and **Ray McVinnie** — I'm lucky to have access to your depth of knowledge and experience with food.

My husband **Mike** — your love, support and gentle acceptance of me for who I am means everything.

Belinda Foster — You are one of life's truly good people. We are so in sync! I'm indebted to the energy and care you put in behind the scenes.

Booksellers — seeing my books on your shelves will always be magic. Thank you for the love you give the books of the world.

To my beloved *four* **parents** whom I love in infinite amounts, and my **close family and friends** — thanks for your unconditional love, support and guidance. Especially **Dana**, for being my soundboard and honest, loving critic.

I wish I had more space for more names because I have a lot of love for a lot of people — but you all **know who you are**.

index